# T
# CA

## AND THE
# YUCATAN

NICK RIDER

EYEWITNESS TRAVEL

Left **Codz Poop (Palace of Masks), Kabah** Center **Ek-Balam** Right **Tin-roofed house, San Felipe**

LONDON, NEW YORK,
MELBOURNE, MUNICH AND DELHI
www.dk.com

Produced by Blue Island, London

Reproduced by Colourscan, Singapore

Printed and bound by South China Printing Co. Ltd., China

First American Edition, 2003
09 10 11 10 9 8 7 6 5 4 3 2 1

Published in the United States by DK Publishing, 375 Hudson Street, New York, New York 10014



Published in Great Britain by Dorling Kindersley Limited

A Catalog record for this book is available from the Library of Congress

ISSN 1479-344X
ISBN 978-0-75664-097-2

Within each Top 10 list in this book, no hierarchy of quality or popularity is implied. All 10 are, in the editor's opinion, of roughly equal merit.



# Contents

## Yucatán's Top 10



**The information in this DK Eyewitness Top 10 Travel Guide is checked regularly.**

Every effort has been made to ensure that this book is as up-to-date as possible at the time of going to press. Some details, however, such as telephone numbers, opening hours, prices, gallery hanging arrangements and travel information are liable to change. The publishers cannot accept responsibility for any consequences arising from the use of this book, nor for any material on third party websites, and cannot guarantee that any website address in this book will be a suitable source of travel information. We value the views and suggestions of our readers very highly. Please write to: Publisher, DK Eyewitness Travel Guides, Dorling Kindersley, 80 Strand, London, Great Britain WC2R 0RL.

Cover: Front – **4Corners Images:** SIME/Schmid Reinhard c; **Hemispheres Images**: Bertrand Gardel main. Spine – **DK Images:** Linda Whitwam b. Back – **DK Images:** Demetrio Carrasco cla; Linda Whitwam ca, cra.

Left **Mayan ruins tour** Centre **Hotel Zone, Cancún** Right **Waterside restaurants, Cancún**



## Around the Yucatán



## Streetsmart

Left **Xcaret Mayan Village** Right **Campeche**

***Key to abbreviations***

**Adm** *admission charge payable* **Air con** *air conditioning* ***C/*** *calle (road)*

PARQUE ECOARQUEOLOGICO

*El Lugar de los Vientos*

## REGLAMENTACION DEL PARQUE

- Nade bajo su propio riesgo.
- Para nadar sugerimos rentar un chaleco salvavidas.
- Para poder nadar ud. deberá darse una ducha.
- No se permite bajar al cenote: Comida, o bebida, ni fumar.
- No nos hacemos responsables por ningún objeto olvidado en el parque.
- No jalar las raíces dentro del agua.
- Prohibo nadar en estado de ebriedad.

LA GERENCIA

CHICHEN, ITZA, YUCATAN, MEXICO

ECOARQUEOLOGICAL PARK

*The Place of the Winds*

## PARK - REGULATIONS

- Swim at your own risk.
- In order to swim- We sugest that you rent a lifejacket.
- Take a shower, before swiming in the cenote.
- Help us to keep the enviroment clean.
- Do not take food or beverages into the cenote and do not smoke.
- We are not responsible for any objects left in the park.
- Do not touch the roots, in the cenote.
- Forbidden to swim if you drank any alcoholic beverage.

THE MANAGEMENT

CHICHEN, ITZA, YUCATAN, MEXICO

# THE YUCATÁN'S TOP 10



THE YUCATÁN'S TOP 10

# TOP 10 Highlights of the Yucatán

*Mexico's Yucatán Peninsula has a special atmosphere and an immense variety of attractions, including some of the world's best beaches and diving areas. The modern, glittering resorts of the east coast's "Mayan Riviera" lie alongside charming old Spanish Colonial towns, sleepy Mayan villages, and the awesome remains of ancient civilizations.*

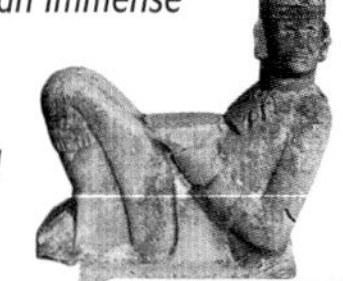

**Chacmool, Chichén Itzá**

## 1 Cancún

Mexico's biggest resort has 23 km (14 miles) of dazzling white sand beaches, lavish hotels, every kind of restaurant, and attractions from water parks to giant nightclubs for 24-hour entertainment *(see pp8–9)*.

## 2 Cozumel

The divers' favorite, with over 20 coral reefs that are enjoyed by first-time snorkelers and experienced divers alike. Onshore there are fine beaches and gleaming jewelry stores *(see pp10–11)*.

## 3 Playa del Carmen

The trendiest spot on the Riviera, with a more small-town scale than Cancún, superb swimming and snorkeling, and an ever-buzzing nightlife *(see pp12–15)*.

## 4 Isla Mujeres

A laid-back Caribbean island with a beachcomber style. It is surrounded by rich diving reefs and fishing grounds *(see pp16–17)*.

Previous pages **The Mayan ruins of Tulum**

## 5 Tulum

Here, one of the most spectacular Mayan ruins perches on a crag overlooking palm-lined sands and relaxed *cabaña* hotels *(see pp18–19)*.

## 6 Sian Ka'an Reserve

This almost uninhabited expanse of lakes, reefs, lagoon, mangroves, and forest is home to jaguars, monkeys, and millions of birds and rare plants *(see pp20–21)*.

## 7 Chichén Itzá

The most awe-inspiring of all Mayan cities, Chichén's pyramids loom over huge plazas, intricately aligned with the movements of the sun and stars *(see pp22–5)*.

## 8 Mérida

Charming squares, shady patios, whitewashed façades, and wonderful markets make this one of the most romantic of all Mexico's historic Colonial cities *(see pp26–7)*.

## 9 Uxmal

The pyramids, palaces, and quadrangles of this dramatic ruined city have a special elegance and beauty, and are regarded by many as the pinnacle of ancient Mayan architecture *(see pp28–31)*.

## 10 Campeche

The city is a remarkable survivor from the Spanish Colonial era. It includes an old section ringed by ramparts and bastions, and an astonishing museum of Mayan relics housed in an ancient fortress *(see pp34–5)*.

# TOP 10 Cancún

*Just a dot on the map before 1970, Cancún is now the biggest resort on the Caribbean. Its Hotel Zone occupies a huge, narrow sand spit shaped like a giant "7." On the mainland is the fast-growing city of Ciudad Cancún – also known as Downtown. All along Boulevard Kukulcán are hotels, shopping malls, restaurants, and visitor attractions.*

*The spit at dusk*

**Kilometer markers, numbered from the north end, are used as locators along Boulevard Kukulcán.**

**Bus routes R-1, R-2 and R-15 run up and down between Avenida Tulum and along the Hotel Zone, 24 hours a day.**

**For good Mexican cooking and some local atmosphere, try the restaurants inside Mercado 28 in Downtown Cancún.**

- *Map H2 & R2–S2*
- *Tourist info kiosks inside Town Hall, Av Tulum, La Isla and Forum malls, and Centro de Convenciones, (998) 881 9000; www.cancun.info*
- *El Rey ruins, 8am–5pm daily; adm $3*
- *El Meco ruins, 8am–5pm daily; adm $3*
- *Museo de Antropología e Historia, 8am–5pm daily; adm $3*

## Top 10 Sights

1. Night-time Cancún
2. The Beach
3. Laguna Nichupté
4. Punta Cancún and the "Corazone"
5. Museo de Antropología e Historia
6. Shopping Areas
7. Avenida Tulum and Downtown
8. El Meco Ruins
9. El Rey Ruins
10. Parque Nizuc

### 1 Night-time Cancún

Cancún's pulsating night-life is most concentrated in the "Corazone" but extends all the way to Ciudad Cancún. A non-stop party atmosphere is maintained in clubs varying from Mexican traditional to modern cool.

### 2 The Beach

Cancún's greatest glory is made up of fine white silicate sand that's soft and somehow always cool despite the warmth of the sun. There are several public access points from Boulevard Kukulcán. The north side of the "7" is best for swimming; the eastern beaches have more crashing waves.

**Northside beach at Cancún**

### 3 Laguna Nichupté

The placid lagoon enclosed by Cancún Island offers more tranquillity than the ocean, and is a favorite place for water sports. To the west are mangroves and jungle *(below)*.

### 4 Punta Cancún and the "Corazone"

The heart of the action on the Hotel Zone strip *(above)* is around the bend in the "7." Here are vast shopping and entertainment malls, such as Plaza Caracol and Forum by the Sea, and the biggest nightclubs, Dady'O and the Coco Bongo *(see p81)*.

## 6 Shopping Areas

Cancún is a shopaholic's heaven. You have everything from international fashion in the vast, gleaming malls *(above left)* of the Hotel Zone to Mexican souvenirs in the markets of Downtown.

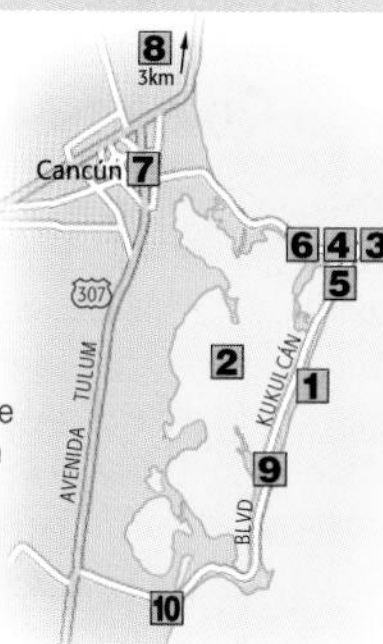


## 5 Museo de Antropología e Historia

The star exhibit is a 15th-century stucco head known as The King (El Rey). The deliberately misshapen human skulls show the Mayan ideals of beauty.

## 7 Avenida Tulum and Downtown

The hub of the more Mexican town of Ciudad Cancún is tree-lined Avenida Tulum. It's a good spot for strolling and souvenir-shopping, and its cafés and restaurants are more tranquil than those by the beach.

## 8 El Meco Ruins

Near the Isla Mujeres ferry ports, the ruined city of El Meco dates back to AD 300 *(above)*. An impressive pyramid and the remains of an opulent Mayan palace can be seen.

## 9 El Rey Ruins

These ruins *(right)* were part of a city that was prominent in the last centuries of Mayan civilization, just before the Spanish Conquest. By the ruins is a mock Mayan village, presenting a reconstruction of ancient Mayan life, including traditional cooking.

## 10 Parque Nizuc

The giant theme park combines slides and rides of all sizes at the Wet'n' Wild water park *(left)*; a snorkeling pool with stingrays and (harmless) sharks; an interactive dolphin pool; and bungee-jumping from the Sky Coaster *(see also p58)*.

### A Growing Resort

The Camino Real hotel by the tip of Punta Cancún is where Cancún all started back in 1971, when it opened as the first hotel on the island. The rest of the "7" was then empty except for trees, dunes, and a very few beach houses and fishing lodges. Since then, Cancún has acquired over 25,000 hotel beds.

*For more on Cancún and the northern part of the Mayan Riviera* **see pp74–83**

# Top 10 Cozumel

*The island of Cozumel was the first part of the Yucatán to be "discovered" for modern visitors when, in the 1950s, the famous ocean explorer Jacques Cousteau came here. Second only to the Great Barrier Reef in the scale of its coral reef system, Cozumel was declared by Cousteau to be one of the finest diving areas in the world. The island's offshore reef is full of life and a dazzling array of colors. Onshore, Cozumel has an easygoing atmosphere, ideal for families.*

Church, San Miguel

*San Miguel Harbor*

**The waters off Cozumel are so clear and some reefs so close to the surface that you can often see as much by snorkeling or free-diving as you can by using scuba equipment.**

**Some of the most atmospheric places to eat are the restaurants scattered along the wild east coast of Cozumel.**

- *Map H3–4 & R5*
- *Parque Chankanaab, 8am–6pm daily; adm $12, discount for under 12s; snorkel hire extra,*
- *San Gervasio ruins, 7am–4pm daily; adm $5, under 12s free*
- *Parque Punta Sur, 8am–5pm daily; adm $10, under 8s free*
- *Museo de Cozumel, 9am–5pm daily; adm $3*
- *Cozumel Parks, (987) 872 2940*
- *Tourist information, (987) 872 7585; www.islacozumel.com.mx*

## Top 10 Sights

1. San Miguel
2. Museo de Cozumel
3. North Beach Hotel Zone
4. Paraíso Reef
5. Laguna Chankanaab
6. Playa Mia and Playa San Francisco
7. Palancar Reef
8. Parque Punta Sur
9. Punta Santa Cecilia and Chen Río
10. San Gervasio Ruins

### 1 San Miguel

Cozumel's only town has a laid-back streetlife centered on the waterfront (Malecón) and Plaza Cozumel. For shoppers, there's the new and very lavish Punta Langosta mall and cruise terminal *(see p92)*.

### 2 Museo de Cozumel

Cozumel's charming waterfront museum in San Miguel illuminates the history of Mayan Cozumel, the arrival of the Spaniards, and the dawn of the pirate era. It also has a lovely rooftop café *(see p94)*.

Parque Punta Sur

### 3 North Beach Hotel Zone

The island's biggest upscale hotel cluster is situated along a shaded boulevard north of town. Multistory hotels and resort complexes line a row of intimate beaches *(left)*. Pools, water sports, and every comfort are on hand, and there are fine views across the channel to the Yucatán mainland from most hotel rooms.

## 4 Paraíso Reef

Shallow and close to the shore, this is a favorite reef for snorkeling, beginners' scuba courses, and easy diving by day and night. Parrot fish are common.

## 5 Laguna Chankanaab

Created around a natural coral lagoon, this glorious park *(above)* includes a botanical garden, a dolphin pool, a pretty beach, and reefs that are ideal for novice divers.

## 6 Playa Mia and Playa San Francisco

Two of Cozumel's best beaches *(Playa Mia below)*, packed with facilities for water lovers, from banana boat rides to subaqua exploration.

## 7 Palancar Reef

The most famous of Cozumel's reefs, with fabulous coral canyons and caves in livid reds and blues. The waters are full of vibrant creatures, including the luminous angelfish *(see p47)*.

## 8 Parque Punta Sur

A wildly diverse nature reserve, with turtle-nesting beaches, a snorkeling area, and huge mangroves and lagoons that are home to crocodiles and flamingos. There's also a lighthouse and a tiny Mayan temple.

## 9 Punta Santa Cecilia and Chen Río

The east side of the island is more rugged and windblown than the west, with rocky, empty beaches and crashing surf that can be dangerous to swim in. At Punta Santa Cecilia there's a lonely beach bar, Mezcalito's, which has great views, while Chen Río has a lovely sheltered beach and an idyllic beach restaurant *(see p70)*.

## 10 San Gervasio Ruins

Cozumel's Mayan capital was one of the richest religious and trading cities in pre-Conquest Yucatán. The layout of its pyramids and small palaces gives a strong impression of life in a Mayan community.

### Mayan Cozumel

As a shrine to Ixchel, goddess of fertility, Cozumel was one of the most important places of pilgrimage in the Yucatán in the centuries just before the Spanish Conquest *(see p37)*. A visit here was seen as especially important for childless women, though everyone in Mayan Yucatán tried to make the trip at least once in their lives.

# Top 10 Playa del Carmen

*If you prefer a beach-town atmosphere to the long hotel strip of Cancún, this is the ideal choice on the Mayan Riviera. Only a tiny fishing village with sand streets in the 1980s, and a backpackers' hang-out in the early '90s, Playa has blossomed into a fun town with an energetic beach- and nightlife.*

*Quinta Avenida*

**Take your own snorkels. They're expensive to rent or buy in Playa.**

**For good traditional Mexican food at lower prices, eat away from the Quinta. Along Calle 4 there are several enjoyable, low-key restaurants with bargain seafood, like Las Brisas** ***(see p83).***

- *Map H3 & Q4*
- *Tourist information: Av 20 and 1ª sur; (984) 873 0242; www.playadelcarmen.caribemexicano.com; 9am–8:30pm Mon–Fri, 9am–5pm Sat, Sun*
- *Xcaret, (998) 883 3143, www.xcaretcancun.com; summer: 9am–10pm, winter: 9am–9pm; tours daily from Cancún and Playa del Mar, adm $59–72, children 5–12 $29–36 (under 5s free)*

## Top 10 Sights

1. Town Beach
2. Quinta Avenida
3. Nighttime Playa
4. Hip Hotels
5. Xaman-Ha Mayan Ruins
6. Playacar
7. Playacar Aviary
8. Playa Tukán and Mamita's Beaches
9. Chunzubul Beach
10. Xcaret

### 1 Town Beach

Center of the action by day is the main beach *(above)*, with more beautiful soft, white Yucatán sand and plenty of shoreline cafés. Beach volleyball is something of a specialty.

### 2 Quinta Avenida

Stretching north from the town plaza, "Fifth Avenue" is Playa's main drag, for daytime shopping and nighttime promenading. Spread along the pedestrianized avenue is a multicolored array of shops, cafés, hotels, clubs, and pavement restaurants.

### 3 Nighttime Playa

After dark the Quinta buzzes with wandering crowds meeting up, dining and bar-hopping. With mariachi bands in some bars and techno DJs in others, there's plenty of variety. The center of the action is the junction of the Quinta and Calle 12.

**Beachfront at Playa**

### 4 Hip Hotels

Playa is well known for its stylish small hotels, like Mosquito Blue on Calle 12, El Faro, and especially Deseo *(below, see also p127)*. Discreetly spectacular and with wonderful pools, they showcase contemporary elegance.

## 5 Xaman-Ha Mayan Ruins

Playa shares its ground with the site of a Mayan settlement known as Xaman-Ha *(below)*. Several temples survive, most scattered around the Playacar area.

## 6 Playacar

This smartly landscaped development *(above)* shows a different side of Playa. It encompasses resort hotels, winding lanes of luxury villas, a fine aviary, Mayan ruins, beach clubs, restaurants, and a championship standard golf course *(see p56)*.

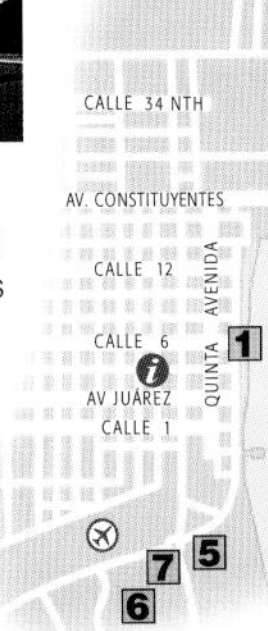

## 7 Playacar Aviary

The aviary within Playacar *(above)* contains a fine collection of toucans, parrots, flamingos, and over 50 other bird species in a lush green setting that seems almost like real jungle. A very easy way to see some of the Yucatán's rarer birds without trekking into the forest.

## 8 Playa Tukán and Mamita's Beach

Two beach clubs, with laid-back bar-restaurants, palapa-sunshades and loungers for hire, and snorkel tours. The hotels nearby all have arrangements so that guests can use the beach-club facilities free of charge.

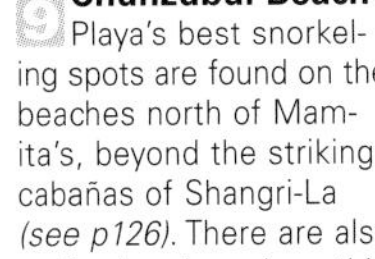

## 9 Chunzubul Beach

Playa's best snorkeling spots are found on the beaches north of Mamita's, beyond the striking cabañas of Shangri-La *(see p126)*. There are also nudist beaches along this stretch of coast.

## 10 Xcaret

Created around a natural lagoon 6 km (4 miles) south of Playa, Xcaret is a huge, imaginatively landscaped "eco-park" bursting with flora, fauna, and sea life *(see pp14–15)*. *Map G3 & Q4*

### The Beach Bar League

Unswervingly popular and the hub of the local scene ever since it first opened back in the days when Playa was just a village under palm trees, the Blue Parrot *(see pp60–61)* was voted "one of the world's ten best beach bars" in an international magazine survey of the late '90s. The judges must have enjoyed their research.

*For diving and snorkeling in the reefs off Playa* **see pp46 & 124**

Left **Mayan Village** Center **Ball Court** Right **Mariposario butterfly garden**

# Playa del Carmen: Xcaret

**Snorkeling river**

### 1 Underground Snorkeling River

This winding stream of clear turquoise water allows you to swim and snorkel all the way through the park and the Mayan village to the beach, via rocky canyons, pools, and caverns lit by shafts of daylight.

### 2 Dolphin Pools

Xcaret has two pools by the beach where visitors can swim with friendly dolphins. It's an extremely popular activity, and only a few people are allowed into the pools each day, so pre-book or try to reserve a slot as soon as you arrive at the park.

### 3 Sea Trek

A fabulous guided walk – not swim – right along the seabed, using weights to keep you from floating upwards and simple breathing apparatus. You don't need to be a great swimmer to enjoy this, and on the way you see all kinds of wonderful sea life from below.

### 4 La Caleta Cove and Blue Lagoon

Fine places for easy swimming. La Caleta ("the Inlet") was the main harbor of Mayan Polé and is now a favorite snorkeling spot, with coral and tropical fish just below the surface. The Blue Lagoon is a big, ultra-relaxing clearwater pool behind the beach, with islands of thick vegetation inviting exploration.

### 5 Mayan Village and Ball Court

Reached via atmospheric passageways, the village endeavors to represent some of the life of the ancient Mayan world. This includes a reconstruction of a Mayan ball court, where a modern interpretation of the mysterious, long-lost ball game *(see p25)* is played each afternoon. There's also a well-presented museum by the park entrance.

***Note**: there are extra charges for the dolphin pools, Sea Trek and snorkel hire*

Turtle pool

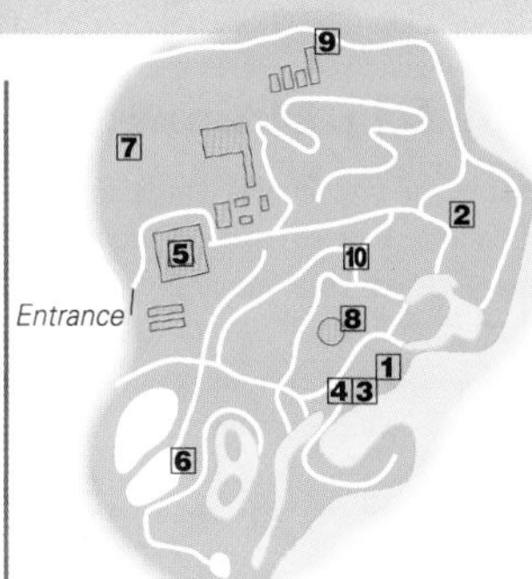


## 6 Butterfly Garden

One of the most spectacular parts of Xcaret, the *mariposario* is the largest butterfly garden in the world, part-hidden in a steep ravine beneath a giant net of a roof. Bursting with all manner of exuberant tropical flowers and vegetation, the garden is alive with an astonishing variety of colorful butterflies. Mornings are best.

## 7 Aviary and Zoo

Animal attractions are spread all around the park. Among the birds on view – all native to the Yucatán – are toucans, cute aracaris or "little toucans," bright green parrots, and very rare birds like the quetzal, whose spectacular tail feathers were once used in the headdresses of Mayan lords. Animals include spider monkeys, bats, and pumas.

## 8 Turtle Pools

Near La Caleta, you can see different kinds of sea turtles – hawksbills, loggerheads, and leatherbacks – in every stage of life, from newborns to grumpy-faced ancients with beautiful shells over 1 m (3 ft) long. The pools are part of a repopulation program to preserve this endangered species.

Parrot

## 9 Forest Trail and Orchid Greenhouse

A well-signposted trail helps you explore many other parts of the park, through lush natural forest and passing further attractions, such as beehives, animal enclosures, a mushroom farm, and a wonderful greenhouse with more than 100 magnificent varieties of rare orchid. You can also explore a longer, guided trail on horseback.

## 10 Live Show

Presented nightly, this is a spectacular mix of entertainment spread around the village and theater. It begins with a *charrería*, or Mexican rodeo, and goes on through "ancient Mayan" rituals to mariachis and vibrant performances of folk music and dances from all over Mexico.

Live show

# Top 10 Isla Mujeres

*Site of the first Spanish landing in Mexico in 1517, "Island of Women" takes its name from the idols of the goddess Ixchel found here. Though close to Cancún, the island has a laid-back atmosphere and has long been a backpackers' favorite. It also has excellent diving and fishing opportunities.*

Dolphin Discovery

*Isla town*

**The slow ferry from Puerto Juárez to Isla is the cheapest and nicest ride.**

**Rent a golf cart, scooter, or bicycle to see the whole island.**

**Gather food for a picnic at Isla Town before touring the island.**

- *Map H2, S1 & L1–2*
- *Tourist office: Av Rueda Medina 130, to the left from the ferry quay; (998) 877 0307; www.cancunmexico.com.mx; 9am–4pm Mon–Fri*
- *Dolphin Discovery, (998) 849 4757; www.dolphindiscovery.com; adm $125 (swimming with dolphins), $165–$195 (dive); minimum age 8 years; reservations essential*
- *Hacienda Mundaca, 9am–6pm daily adm $2*
- *Parque Garrafón, (998) 877 1100; summer: 8:30am–6:30pm daily, winter: 8:30am–5pm daily; adm $29–$59*
- *Parque Escultórico Punta Sur, 7am–10pm daily; free*

## Top 10 Sights

1. Isla Town
2. Playa Norte
3. Playa Secreto
4. Dolphin Discovery
5. Hacienda Mundaca
6. El Garrafón
7. Parque Escultórico Punta Sur
8. Manchones Reef
9. Sleeping Sharks Cave
10. Isla Contoy

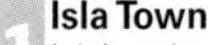

### 1 Isla Town

Isla's only town still has the look of a Caribbean fishing village, with narrow, sandy streets and wooden houses painted in bright pinks, yellows, greens, and blues. There are plenty of cafés and souvenir shops, and few cars.

### 2 Playa Norte

This beach *(above)* at the northern tip of the town is the place where many Isla visitors spend their days, with laid-back beach bars like Buho's *(see p82)* for refreshment breaks. With pure white sand and calm turquoise waters, it's excellent for tranquil swimming.

Fishing boat on the white sands

### 3 Playa Secreto

To the northeast of Isla town, this "secret" beach *(below)* is in a sheltered inlet that's even more shallow and placid than Playa Norte, and is wonderful for small children. A footbridge across it leads to the Avalon Grand resort.

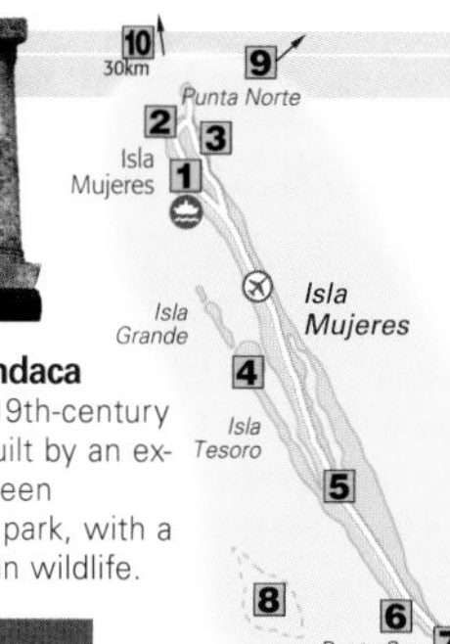


### 4 Dolphin Discovery

One of the largest interactive dolphin centers on the Riviera, offering visitors a range of options for swimming and diving with these ultra-friendly creatures. Other Dolphin Discovery centers are at Cozumel and Puerto Aventuras.

### 5 Hacienda Mundaca

The ruins of a 19th-century mansion *(above)* built by an ex-slave trader have been transformed into a park, with a small zoo of Yucatán wildlife.

### 6 El Garrafón

This nature park and snorkeling center is created around a natural, shallow pool *(below)*. There are restaurants, equipment rental, and swimming and snorkeling opportunities in the rock pool, offshore reefs, or in the swimming pool.

### 7 Parque Escultórico Punta Sur

The southern tip of the island has been transformed into a sculpture park, with striking modern art works *(right)* spread around the wind-blown headland and lighthouse.

### 8 Manchones Reef

Isla Mujeres' most popular reef for scuba courses and easy diving. Only about 10–12 m (30–40 ft) deep, the waters are safe and have plenty of colorful coral and fish to discover.

### 9 Sleeping Sharks Cave

An underground river meets the sea at this cave, attracting sharks that come to bask, trancelike, in the mixture of fresh and salt water. A must-see for experienced divers – but don't wake those sharks!

### 10 Isla Contoy

An uninhabited island about 30 km (18 miles) north of Isla Mujeres, Contoy is an important seabird reserve for pelicans, cormorants, frigate birds, spoonbills, and others. Day trips are run by companies on Isla.

### The Lafittes

Isla Mujeres' most famous residents were the 19th-century Lousiana-born brothers Jean and Pierre Lafitte, considered the last great Caribbean pirates. Sailing southward after falling out with the U.S. Government, they built a stronghold on the Isla lagoon, but were attacked by the Spanish Navy in 1821. Both badly wounded, they escaped in a boat, and Pierre is believed to have died in Dzilam Bravo on the Yucatán mainland. His brother's fate remains a mystery.

# Top 10 Tulum

*One of the Yucatán's most beautiful places, Tulum offers a special combination of spectacular Mayan ruins and miles of superb, palm-lined beaches. Nearby, too, is the finest cave diving area in the world. This is the most popular destination in the Yucatán for finding cabañas – rooms in palm-roofed cabins right by the beach and the waves.*

*Mayan ruin at Tulum*

**Beach cabañas are in demand in peak season, and the cheaper ones are often booked up by 10am each day.**

**The Diamante-K cabañas, north of the T-junction, have a vegetarian café and juice bar, open to non-residents.**

- *Map G4 & P6*
- *Tourist info: (984) 873 1490; www.rivieramaya.com; www.inah.gob.mx*
- *Tulum Ruins, 8am–5pm daily; adm $3*
- *Xel-Ha Park, (984) 883 0524; www.xelha.com.mx; 9am–6pm daily; adm $18–$46, children $9–$23, under 5s free*
- *Dos Ojos/ Hidden Worlds, (984) 877 8535; www.hiddenworlds.com.mx; dive times 9am to 5pm daily; charges per activity, adm $40–$90, plus $15 gear rental*
- *Gran Cenote and Aktun–Ha, sunrise to sunset daily; adm $2*

## Top 10 Sights

1. Tulum Ruins
2. El Castillo
3. Hippy Heaven
4. Secluded Heaven
5. Tulum Pueblo
6. Gran Cenote
7. Aktun-Ha Cenote
8. Tankah
9. Dos Ojos Cenote
10. Xel-Ha

**Tulum beach**

### 1 Tulum Ruins

Mayan Tulum was a walled town and prosperous trading community at the time when the Spaniards arrived in the 1520s. The ruins *(above)* include a recognizable main street, the Palace of the Halach Uinic, and the House of the Columns.

### 2 El Castillo

The most impressive of the Mayan buildings at Tulum is the great temple-pyramid *(below)*. A flaming beacon at the top of the temple was once visible for miles.

## 3 Hippy Heaven

The oldest and simplest cabaña clusters – Don Armando's, the Mar Caribe – are along the stretch of the beach road close to the ruins. Don't come here if you want much privacy or more than basic showers and other facilities.

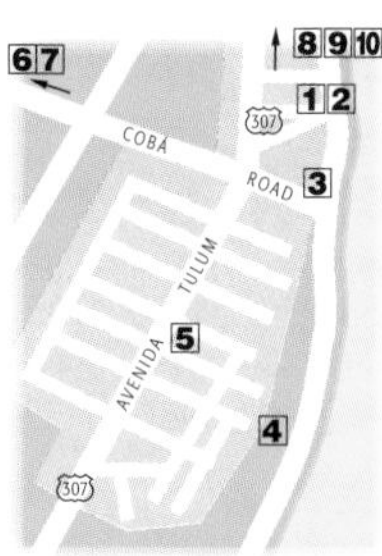


## 4 Secluded Heaven

Along the stretch of beach *(left)* south of the T-junction in the road is a wide choice of beach cabins, from plain stick-and-sand-floor huts to luxurious cabañas, most of them secluded. Few have electricity and are lit only by candles at night.

## 5 Tulum Pueblo

The village of Tulum is a rambling place spread out along the main highway. Almost 100 per cent Mayan just a few years ago, it now has a bank, bus terminus, cafés, small hotels, and backpacker services.

## 6 Gran Cenote

Along the road toward Cobá from Tulum are several accessible cenotes. The Gran Cenote is one of the most attractive for swimmers and snorkelers, surrounded by rock columns and exotic flowers, and leading into a wide, arching cavern.

## 7 Aktun-Ha Cenote

Another enjoyable cenote for swimming, with a broad, peaceful pool that runs into a dark and mysterious cave system. As you swim around the pool you see many shoals of tiny fish.

### Cenotes

The Yucatán Peninsula is a vast slab of limestone riddled with labyrinths of caves and subterranean rivers. Water is accessible only through natural sinkholes in the rock, called *cenotes* in Spanish. These vary from tiny wells to cathedral-like caverns. Their water, fed by underground springs, is always cool and fresh. Swimming in cenotes is one of the unforgettable Yucatán experiences, and the Tulum area is a center for cave diving.

## 8 Tankah

A bumpy, winding road leads to this little-developed beach which has an enjoyable beach-bar and restaurant, and a large, easily swimmable cenote just inland of the track.

## 9 Dos Ojos Cenote

This cenote is the entrance to the world's longest known underwater cave system, which stretches over 600 km (350 miles). The Hidden Worlds Center *(see p51)* offers exhilarating tours.

## 10 Xel-Ha

The coral inlet *(above)* has been landscaped as a snorkel park, plus forest trail and beach. It has plenty of colorful fish and is great for children. Across the highway is a ruined Mayan city.

# Sian Ka'an Biosphere Reserve

*The empty jungle and vast wetlands of Sian Ka'an (Mayan for "where the sky is born") contrast strikingly with the resorts of the Mayan Riviera. Extending south from Tulum around Ascensión Bay, the area encompasses lagoons, reefs, lakes, mangroves, and forests. It is virtually uninhabited and contains a dazzling variety of animal and plant life.*

Flamingos

*Lake Chunyaxché*

**The operators listed below sometimes offer specialist tours, such as snorkeling, bird-watching, or looking for crocodiles at night.**

**Tours tend to include refreshments of some kind (drinks and sandwiches usually), but if you're traveling independently, eat or buy food at Punta Allen.**

- *Map F5–6*
- *Entry to the reserve is $2 per person, but to see the best of the wildlife it is worth joining an eco-friendly tour*
- *Amigos de Sian Ka'an, Cancún; www.amigosdesiankaan.org; tours cost $70 per person*
- *Centro Ecológico Sian Ka'an, (984) 871 2499; www.cesiak.org*
- *Sian Ka'an Tours, Tulum; (984) 871 2363*
- *Tours cost from around $95 per person*

## Top 10 Sights

1. Ben-Ha Cenote
2. Boca Paila
3. Lake Chunyaxché
4. Muyil Ruins
5. Lake Islands
6. Punta Allen
7. Ascension Bay Bonefishing Flats
8. Mangroves and Forest
9. Native and Migratory Birds
10. Animals

### 1 Ben-Ha Cenote

By the warden's lodge at the reserve's entrance, a path leads to a clear, cool cenote *(above)*, where you can swim among reeds and forest trees.

### 2 Boca Paila

Set on a glorious lagoon *(below)*, the Boca Paila Fishing Lodge is a favorite among serious fishermen. This is also where Sian Ka'an tours switch from vans to boats.

Muyil ruins

### 3 Lake Chunyaxché

Sian Ka'an has many lakes that., like all those in the Yucatán, are fed not by rivers but by underground streams. In the channels into Lake Chunyaxché from the lagoon are extraordinary points where the sea and lake waters meet, bringing together a teeming mix of plant life and fish.

## 4 Muyil Ruins

The ruined Mayan city of Muyil lies just outside the reserve. A very old city possibly allied to Cobá *(see p89)*, it has an unusual great pyramid with a building at its top containing several rooms. Beside the ruins, a path leads to Lake Chunyaxché.

## 5 Lake Islands

There are at least 27 Mayan ruins within the reserve, many of them small temples sited on islands in the lakes. It is thought that these lake island temples were probably places of pilgrimage, visited in order to perform special rituals.

## 6 Punta Allen

It is said that this sleepy lobster-fishing village, with its sand streets, big beach *(above)*, and just a few restaurants and places to stay, was founded by Blackbeard the Pirate, whose ship was called *The Allen*.

## 7 Ascension Bay Bonefishing Flats

These shallows are one of the finest flyfishing areas in the world, above all for bonefish. Fishing lodges along the road and Punta Allen's guest houses offer trips out to them.

## 8 Mangroves and Forest

A mix of salt and fresh water at Sian Ka'an provides the ideal conditions for mangroves *(right)*, which are home to two kinds of crocodile. Further inland are large expanses of rain forest and grasslands.

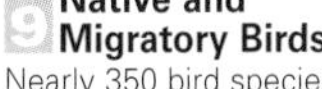

## 9 Native and Migratory Birds

Nearly 350 bird species have been logged as native to Sian Ka'an, and around a million migratory birds visit each year from North America. Among those easiest to see are ibises, egrets, orioles, storks *(right)*, and the American heron.

## 10 Animals

Sian Ka'an is home to every kind of wild cat found in Mexico and Central America, including ocelots and pumas, as well as anteaters, manatees, and tapirs. However, you're most likely to see raccoons, bush pigs, spider monkeys, gray foxes, and iguanas.

### Chechen & Chakah

The toxicity of the small chechen tree can make people numb and dizzy by its aroma alone. But if local Maya ever rub against the tree's leaves, they know they have only to look around for a nearby chakah bush to find the natural antidote to the chechen's poison.

*Note: the road to Punta Allen is extremely rough and should be negotiated only in a four-wheel drive vehicle* (see p90)

# TOP 10 Chichén Itzá

*Built to a scale that seems from another world, Chichén, one of the new seven wonders of the world, has some of the largest buildings of the ancient Mayan cities. It had a port near Río Lagartos and grew rich from trading. With a large population, it became the most powerful city in the whole of the Yucatán in the last centuries of the Classic Mayan era (AD 750–950), defeating Cobá, Izamal, and others in war. A visit to these great ruins is not to be missed.*

*Serpent head at foot of the Castillo de Kukulcán*

**To see Chichén at its best, stay nearby the night before and get to the site early, before the main heat of the day and before the arrival of the big crowds from Cancún at about 11am.**

**The little town of Pisté just west of the ruins has several pleasant restaurants along its main street, such as Las Mestizas *(see p103)*, which have more charm than the visitor center at the site itself.**

- *Map E3*
- *8am–5pm daily*
- *Sound and Light Show, winter: 7pm daily, summer: 8pm daily*
- *Adm $8; includes show, but extra charge of $2.50 for English, German, Italian, or French commentary via headphones; www.inah.gob.mx*

## Top 10 Sights

1. Sound and Light Show
2. Castillo de Kukulcán
3. Great Ball Court
4. Sacred Cenote
5. Temple of the Warriors
6. Court of the Thousand Columns
7. High Priest's Grave
8. Observatory
9. Nunnery
10. Old Chichén

### 1 Sound and Light Show

Presented nightly, the show features an imagined history of Chichén Itzá, while the main temples are dramatically lit in changing colors.

### 2 Castillo de Kukulcán

It is no longer possible to climb this awesome pyramid *(right)* which encloses an older one, access to which is from the top of the Castillo. Carvings, panels, levels, and the 365 steps are all symbols of the intricate Mayan calendar.

Castillo de Kukulcán

### 3 Great Ball Court

Built in AD 864, this is the biggest ancient ball court in Mexico *(see p25)*. It has exceptional carvings *(left)* and remarkable acoustics – a normal voice can be heard from each end of the court.



*For Chichén Itzá's best carvings and more about the ancient Mayan ball game* **see pages 24–5**

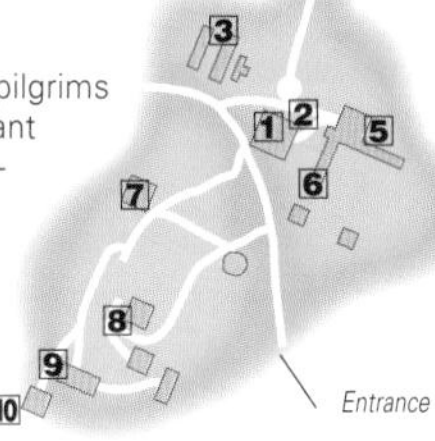


### 4 Sacred Cenote

Visited by Mayan pilgrims over centuries, the giant natural cenote or sinkhole *(left; see also p19)*, has yielded jewelry, sculptures, and animal bones.

### 5 Temple of the Warriors

The squat temple opposite the Castillo was used in city rituals. In front of it are ranks of pillars, each intricately carved with portraits of important figures in the Chichén elite *(below)*.

### 6 Court of the Thousand Columns

The forest of pillars around a giant quadrangle once supported wood and palm roofs. This was the main place for doing business in Chichén: for buying, selling, and voicing disputes.

### 7 High Priest's Grave

Almost like a smaller prototype of the later Castillo, this pyramid has an inscription with the date of its completion: June 20, 842. It gets its name from a tomb excavated at its foot, which cannot be visited.

### 8 Observatory

The observatory *(right)* is also called El Caracol ("snail") because of its odd round shape. Three slots in its top level point due south and toward the setting sun and moon on the spring and autumn equinoxes.

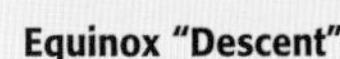

### 9 Nunnery

The Spaniards thought this group of buildings was a nunnery, but experts now believe it formed the main residential and administrative area for Chichén's lords in the city's first years. The buildings are covered in spectacular carvings *(below)*

### 10 Old Chichén

Chichén Itzá covered a much wider area than is seen at the monumental core. A path leads south to Chichén Viejo – a part-excavated site in the woods, which is as old as the central plazas.

### Equinox "Descent"

On the spring equinox, the afternoon sun picks out the tails of the serpents lining the Castillo's north stairway and runs down to their heads just before sunset. On the autumn equinox, the reverse effect occurs. This "Descent of Kukulcán" symbolized the city's contact with the gods. Today, huge crowds flock to see the phenomenon.

*For more Mayan ruins in the Yucatán* **see pp38–9**

Left **Warrior figure** Right **Depictions of Chac, the rain god, on the Nunnery façade**

# TOP 10 Chichén Itzá: The Carvings

## 1 Heads of Kukulcán
The giant feathered serpents at the Castillo probably represented Vision Serpents *(see p37)* but have also been associated with the central Mexican serpent-god Quetzalcoatl.

## 2 Chac Mool and Altar of the Red Jaguar
Reclining Chac Mool figures were fallen warriors delivering offerings to the gods, from food and jewels to the hearts of sacrificial victims. The Chac Mool in the inner temple of the Castillo stands in front of a painted stone jaguar, a symbol of cosmic forces.

## 3 Temple of the Jaguars
Carved panels connect the foundation of Chichén Itzá with First Mother and First Father, the creators of the world.

## 4 Ball Court Frieze
As defeated ball game players have their heads cut off, seven spurts of blood shoot from their necks and are transformed into vines and flowers.

## 5 Tzompantli
Covered in carved skulls on all four sides, a low platform near the Ball Court was probably used to display the heads of sacrificial victims.

**Kukulcán head**

## 6 Platform of the Jaguars and Eagles
This small platform may have been used for rituals by the Orders of the Jaguars and Eagles – special groups of warriors. Its carvings show these animals tearing open human victims to eat their hearts.

## 7 Warriors' Columns
A "picture gallery" of the men of Chichén. Most are of warriors in their battle regalia, but there are also some priests and bound captives.

## 8 Casa Colorada Inscriptions
These record that several lords of Chichén celebrated a ritual here in September 869, to ensure the city's prosperity.

## 9 Chac-Masks of Las Monjas
The curling snout of the rain-god Chac is depicted repeatedly in rows at the Nunnery.

## 10 Snails, Armadillos, Turtles, and Crabs
Placed between the Chac-heads on the Iglesia ("church") at the Nunnery, these animals represented the four spirits that held up the sky at the cardinal points (north, south, east, west) in Mayan mythology.


*For more about the Mayan gods and spirits* **see p37**

# The Ball Game

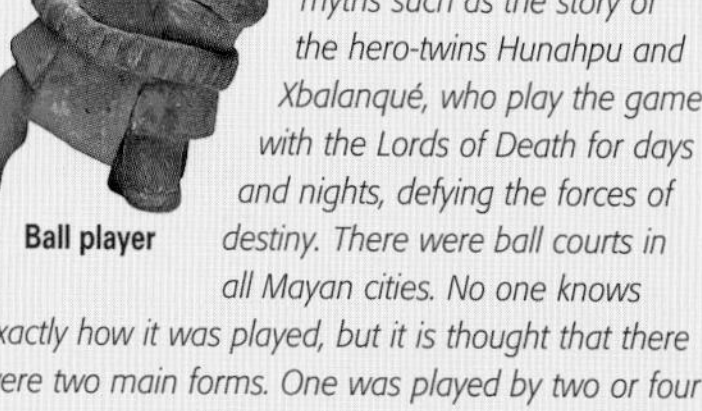

Ball player

*The ancient Mexican ball game can be traced back to before 1500 BC. It features in Mayan myths such as the story of the hero-twins Hunahpu and Xbalanqué, who play the game with the Lords of Death for days and nights, defying the forces of destiny. There were ball courts in all Mayan cities. No one knows exactly how it was played, but it is thought that there were two main forms. One was played by two or four players on the older, smaller courts, and the aim was to keep the ball from touching the ground and get it past your opponent(s) and out at the end of the court. The other form corresponded to much bigger courts, such as at Chichén Itzá, and was played by teams of seven who scored in big rings on either side of the court. In either style players could not touch the ball with hands or feet, but only with shoulders, chest and hips, so scoring was very hard. Games had great ritual significance, and sometimes, but not always, losing players were sacrificed.*

### Top 10 Ancient Mayan Ball Courts

1. Monte Albán, Oaxaca
2. Palenque, Chiapas
3. Toniná, Chiapas
4. Uxmal, Yucatán
5. Chichén Itzá, Yucatán
6. Cobá, Quintana Roo
7. Kohunlich, Quintana Roo
8. Calakmul, southern Campeche
9. Tikal, Guatemala
10. Copán, Honduras

Player in protective clothing

Carved ring in ball court

### The Ball Court

Ball courts were found in every one of the ancient cultures of Mexico and Central America. Though the style and size of the courts varied, they were always I-shaped, as in this Aztec codex illustration *(above)*. The game was viewed as symbolic of the cycle of life, and the court represented the world. While games had important religious significance, it is known that men also placed bets on the results.

# Top 10 Mérida

*The most languidly tropical of Mexico's colonial cities, Mérida is a town of whitewashed façades, Moorish-style Spanish houses with deliciously shady, palm-filled patios, tall and plain 17th-century churches, and an unhurried street life. It is also at the center of the Yucatán's distinctive culture, making it the best place to see and shop for traditional crafts and souvenirs.*

Cathedral

Arch

**Ask for the *Yucatán Today* free magazine at tourist offices. It's an excellent source of useful information, with handy maps.**

**For some of the best lunches in Mérida, head away from the main tourist run up to Paseo Montejo. But note that a few of the city's upmarket eateries close in the evenings.**

- *Map C2*
- *Tourist offices: Teatro Peón Contreras, corner of Calle 60 and 57; Palacio de Gobierno, Plaza Mayor*
- *Tourist Info: (999) 924 9290; www.mayayucatan.com.mx*
- *Palacio del Gobernador, 8am–9pm daily; free*
- *Museo de Antropología e Historia, Palacio Cantón, (999) 923 0557; www.inah.gob.mx; 8am–8pm Tue–Sat, 8am–2pm Sun, closed Mon; adm $4*

## Top 10 Sights

1. Plaza Mayor
2. Cathedral
3. Palacio del Gobernador
4. Casa de Montejo
5. Calle 60
6. Iglesia de Jesús
7. Parque Santa Lucía
8. Market
9. Paseo de Montejo
10. Museo de Antropología

### 1 Plaza Mayor

This spacious square was the heart of the Mayan city of Ti'ho, and so was taken as the hub of the new city by Conquistador Francisco Montejo when he founded Mérida in 1542. The square is still surrounded by the city's main public buildings, while its colonnades and benches under a canopy of giant laurel trees provide favorite meeting places.

### 2 Cathedral

Built between 1562 and 1598, this is the oldest cathedral on the American mainland (in the entire continent, only Santo Domingo in the Dominican Republic is older). Massive and monumental, it was built in the sober style of the Spanish Renaissance, with a soaring façade and few decorative flourishes.

Plaza Mayor

### 3 Palacio del Gobernador

Neighboring the Cathedral, the elegant seat of the Yucatán state government was built in 1892 to replace a Spanish governors' palace. Its patios, open to the public, are decorated with striking murals *(below)* by Fernando Castro Pacheco.

## 4 Casa de Montejo

The astonishing portico of the first Spanish stone house completed in Mérida, built for the Montejos themselves in 1549, bears a very graphic celebration of the Conquest. The rest of the house has since been rebuilt and is now a bank.

## 5 Calle 60

Mérida's main drag for strolling and souvenir shopping *(above)*, running from Plaza Mayor through Parque Hidalgo, another fine square with a clutch of cafés and restaurants.

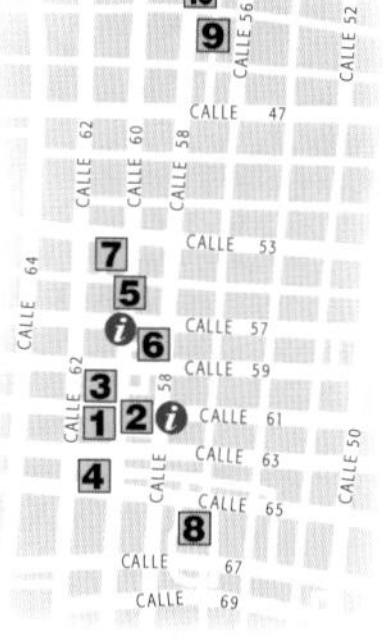

## 6 Iglesia de Jesús

The Jesuits built this church in 1618, favoring ornamentation and a little flair over the plain style of the Franciscans, who built most of the town's other religious buildings.

## 7 Parque Santa Lucía

The arcaded square of Santa Lucía *(above)*, dating in part from 1575, is the most romantic of all Mérida's old squares. Free concerts of traditional music take place every Thursday *(see p63)*.

## 8 Market

Shopping hub of the Yucatán, Mérida's market is a huge bazaar. Stalls are piled high with chilis, fabulous fruit and other food, hammocks, sandals, panama hats, and embroidery *(see p109)*.

## 9 Paseo de Montejo

Laid out in the Yucatán's early 1900s boom in imitation of Parisian boulevards, Paseo de Montejo is lined with lavish mansions, some using fabulous iconography, such as this eagle-and-snake motif.

## 10 Museo de Antropología

The grandest of all the Paseo Montejo mansions, built for General Francisco Cantón between 1909 and 1911, houses one of Mexico's most important archeological museums. It has many treasures excavated from sites all across the Yucatán, and is especially rich in ceramics and jade. Its displays provide an overview of the Mayan world that illuminates visits to the ruins themselves.

### The Tríos

Walk around the Plaza Mayor on most evenings and you'll see groups of men in threes, dressed in white shirts and black trousers, and carrying guitars. These are the Yucatán tríos, traditional troubadours available for hire to play romantic serenades. They can be hired to entertain at a party or wedding, or you can have them sing right there on the square.

# Top 10 Uxmal

*The most majestic of the ruined Mayan cities, Uxmal (which means "three-times-built,") was a powerful city-state from AD 700 to 920. Its spectacular buildings are strikingly like gigantic stage sets and have been compared to the famous monuments of Greece and Rome.*

*House of the Turtles*

**Arrive at the site early in the day to miss the heat and the crowds. Allow at least a full morning to see the whole site.**

**Hal-Tun, beside the road about 2 km (1 mile) north of the ruins, is a charming traditional Yucatecan restaurant with an airy, relaxing terrace.**

- *Map C4*
- *Site 8am–5pm daily*
- *Sound and Light Show, winter: 7pm daily, summer: 8pm daily*
- *Adm $9 Mon–Sat; give tip for the guided visit, plus $2.50 for English, French, German, or Italian commentary; www.inah.gob.mx.*

## Top 10 Sights

1. Pyramid of the Magician
2. Nunnery Quadrangle
3. Ball Court
4. House of the Turtles
5. Governor's Palace
6. Great Pyramid
7. House of the Old Woman
8. House of the Pigeons
9. Temple of the Centipede and the Arch
10. Sound and Light Show

### 1 Pyramid of the Magician

Unusually, Uxmal's best-known pyramid *(below)* has rounded corners. The temple at the top is the legendary home of the Dwarf of Uxmal. Sadly, visitors can no longer climb to the top.

**Pyramid of the Magician**

### 2 Nunnery Quadrangle

This elegant, four-building complex was Uxmal's heart of power and ritual. It was so named by a Spanish friar merely because it reminded him of a convent. Intricate carvings *(below, see also p30)* symbolize the magical authority of the city and its rulers and their contact with the gods.

### 3 Ball Court

Uxmal's main Ball Court is smaller than the Great Court at Chichén Itzá *(see p22)*. The original scoring rings are inscribed with dates from the year 901; those you actually see at the court are replicas.

### 4 House of the Turtles

This delicately proportioned small temple-residence is considered the archetype of the pure Puuc architectural style *(see p31)*. The name comes from its decorative cornice, featuring a line of turtles carved in stone. This is a motif that you will see many times at Uxmal; it was associated with the rebirth of new life and the fertility of the coming of the rains.

*For more on Uxmal's amazing carvings* **see p30**

## 5 Governor's Palace

Often regarded as the finest of all Mayan buildings, this huge palace, over 100 m (300 ft) long, was built for the greatest of Uxmal's rulers, known as Chan-Chak-Kaknal-Ahaw, or Lord Chak. Its huge frieze *(left)* symbolizes time and the cycles of rain, sun, and rebirth.

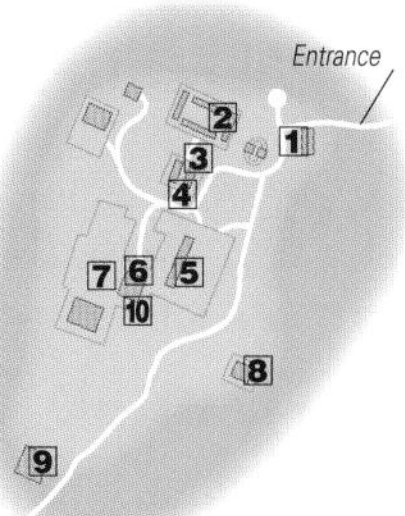

## 6 Great Pyramid

Most of this towering pyramid *(below)* is older than the Governor's Palace next door. Like many Mayan buildings, it was altered and added to many times.

## 7 House of the Old Woman

Only partly excavated, this large pyramid with a Puuc-style temple on one side is among the oldest major structures at Uxmal, dating from about 700. In legend, it is said to be the home of the Dwarf's Mother.

## 9 Temple of the Centipede and the Arch

Unexcavated parts of Uxmal include the Temple of the Centipede. The *sacbé* (Mayan road) leading to it continued to the allied city of Kabah. An arch marks the boundary of Uxmal's central core.

## 10 Sound and Light Show

Every night, Uxmal's major buildings are dramatically lit up in varying colors, and there is a commentary on Uxmal in history and legend.

## 8 House of the Pigeons

This huge complex incorporates temples and palatial residences. Early travelers thought the lofty roof comb above its central quadrangle looked like dovecotes *(below)*, hence the name. It was once covered in sculptures.

### Uxmal's Dwarf

In Mayan legend, Uxmal was founded by an *alux* (leprechaun) who had defied the authority of a local king. When the king dared the dwarf to build a house, the Pyramid of the Magician appeared overnight. On another day the dwarf built the path to Kabah. The king's last test was that they should both be hit on the head with hammers. The king died, but the dwarf was protected by a magic tortilla and went on to rule Uxmal.

Left **Monstermouth, Pyramid of the Magician** Center **Chac gods** Right **Jaguar throne**

# Uxmal: The Carvings

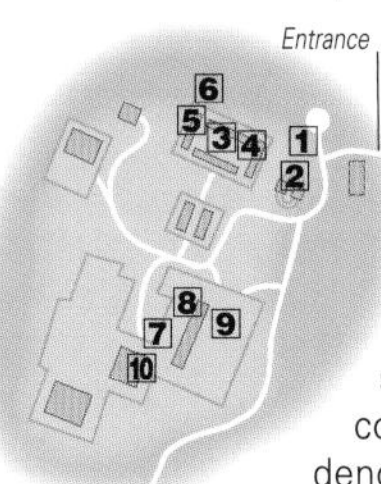


### 1 Monstermouths

Temple entrances in the form of giant monster-like faces, such as on the House of the Dwarf at the Pyramid of the Magician, made a striking connection between a temple and the gods of the earth.

### 2 Birds Quadrangle

Around this small quadrangle are beautiful images of parrots and other birds, which symbolized the unpredictable elements in nature.

### 3 Nunnery Quadrangle: Mayan Huts

A feature of Puuc carving is the combination of complex symbols with everyday images. The huts carved on the Nunnery's South Building are little different from those in Yucatán villages today.

### 4 Nunnery: Vision Serpents

The semi-triangular patterns on the East Building are Vision Serpents – conduits between men and the "Otherworld."

### 5 Nunnery: Serpent Heads

The huge feathered snakes winding around the West Building are probably also Vision Serpents. Human faces emerge from their jaws.

### 6 Nunnery: Flowers and Lattices

Lattice work represented the huts in which meetings were held, while flowers were a symbol of magic. The combination of the two denoted a ceremonial site.

### 7 Muyal Symbols

The simple spiral pattern repeated frequently on the Nunnery and Governor's Palace represents the Mayan word for cloud, *muyal*, another symbol of contact with the heavens.

### 8 Lord Chak

The figure in a spectacular headdress set within the façade of the Governor's Palace is believed to be Lord Chak himself.

### 9 La Picota

The phallic column called the "whipping-post" in Spanish has inscriptions on it that have never been deciphered. It formed part of a fertility cult that was a distinctive feature of Uxmal.

**Governor's Palace**

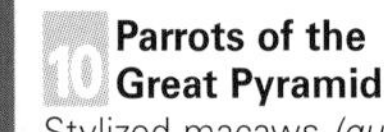

### 10 Parrots of the Great Pyramid

Stylized macaws *(guacamayas)* feature in the carvings on the temple at the top of the Great Pyramid as symbols of uncontrolled nature.

## Top 10 Puuc Cities

1. Oxkintok
2. Uxmal
3. Kabah
4. Sayil
5. Nohpat
6. Xlapak
7. Labná
8. Chacmultún
9. Xcalumkín, Campeche
10. Itzimté, Campeche

# The Puuc Cities

Lord Chac, Kabah's Palace

*Uxmal was the largest of a string of Mayan communities that flourished in the Puuc Hills of southern Yucatán around 650–920. The other well-known ones are Kabah, Sayil, Xlapak, and Labná* (see pp38–9). *Their distinctive style of architecture is the most refined of those used by Mayan builders, characterized by strong horizontal lines, elegant proportions, and a sharp contrast between very plain lower walls and elaborately carved friezes above them. Many architectural details seem to mimic humbler buildings and natural features, such as the small drum columns along the bottom of many Puuc walls, which imitate the stick walls of village huts. The communities that lived in these cities were wealthy but fragile, because this region is one of the driest parts of the Yucatán. Indeed, severe drought was probably a major reason why the southern Mayan cities collapsed very quickly, in AD 920–1000* (see also p36). *A one- or two-day tour of the main Puuc cities is possible, following the recognized Puuc Route, south of Uxmal.*

Snake with a human face between its jaws, Labná

### Kabah's Codz Poop

The main façade of the Codz Poop (Palace of Masks) at Kabah is covered in over 250 faces of the rain-god Chac, whose long, curling snout was even used to form the steps into the palace chambers. The Maya believed that covering structures with images of gods gave the buildings divine powers.

El Mirador, Labná

# TOP 10 Campeche

*The old city of Campeche is a remarkable museum piece of the colonial era. Cobbled streets of aged houses painted in delicate blues, greens, and ochers still sit within the city walls, built to fend off pirate attacks when this was one of the great trading strongholds of the Spanish Empire. Campeche's real museum, housed in an old fortress, displays spectacular Mayan relics from the recently excavated forest city of Calakmul.*

**Jade mask, Fuerte de San Miguel**

*Campeche town center*

**Special "El Guapo" buses run to the fortress museums from the Parque Principal. Otherwise, take a taxi.**

**La Parroquia, just off the Parque Principal at Calle 55 no 8, is a traditional café with excellent breakfasts and great fish dishes.**

- *Map A5*
- *Tourist information: Casa Seis, Parque Principal and Av Ruiz Cortines; (981) 816 6767; www.campeche travel.com*
- *Museo de las Estelas Mayas, 8am–7:30pm*
- *Puerta de Tierra, 9am–8pm; free*
- *Fuerte San Miguel, 8:30am–7:30pm Tue–Sun; adm $2.50*
- *Fuerte San José, 8am–7:30pm Tue–Sun; adm $2.50*
- *Edzná ruins: 8am–5pm; adm $3 Mon–Sat*
- *www.inah.gob.mx*

## Top 10 Sights

1. Parque Principal
2. Cathedral
3. Casa Seis
4. Puerta de Mar
5. Puerta de Tierra
6. Baluarte de Santiago
7. The Malecón
8. Fuerte San Miguel Museum
9. Fuerte San José Museum
10. Edzná

### 1 Parque Principal

Hub of the old town, the broad and airy main square once opened directly onto the waterfront, with landing stages for ships; its 18th-century arcades would have been thronged with sailors and traders. Today, you'll find a pleasant café amid the trees.

**Fuerte de San Miguel**

### 2 Cathedral

Begun in the 1560s, Campeche Cathedral *(left)* was built in many stages and not completed until the 19th century. Its lofty façade, facing the main square, is one of the oldest parts, designed in a Spanish Renaissance style typical of many churches built in the reign of King Philip II.

### 3 Casa Seis

A gracious old house on the west side of the square, restored and furnished to recreate the home of a prosperous 19th-century Campeche merchant. As well as containing a tourist information desk, the house's patio features concerts and exhibitions.

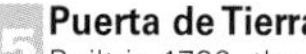

## 4 Puerta de Mar

When the city walls were complete, Puerta de Mar *(right)* provided the only gateway to the harbor. The nearby bastion is now Museo de las Estelas Mayas, displaying Mayan carvings from around Campeche.

## 5 Puerta de Tierra

Built in 1732, the Puerta de Tierra ("Land Gate") was the only way in or out of Campeche on the landward side. Inside it, there is an entertaining museum of maritime and pirate history.

## 6 Baluarte de Santiago

This isolated bastion has been imaginatively used to house a dense and verdant botanical garden, with giant palms and other lush tropical flora.

## 7 The Malecón

The long waterfront has been attractively restored and is a popular place for locals to take an evening stroll. There are often superb sunsets over the Gulf of Mexico.

## 8 Fuerte San Miguel Museum

This former hilltop fortress, 3 km (1.5 miles) south of the city, is now home to a fine collection of Mayan relics, including a set of extraordinarily beautiful jade funeral masks.

## 9 Fuerte San José Museum

Another sturdy Spanish fortress, north of the city *(right)*. It houses the Post-Conquest sections of the town's museum. Wonderful sea and city views from the ramparts.

## 10 Edzná

About 50 km (30 miles) southeast of Campeche, the ruined Mayan city of Edzná rivalled Chichén Itzá and Uxmal in size and wealth. At its heart is the magnificent palace-temple complex, the "Building of the Five Stories" *(left)*, one of the largest and most intricate of all Mayan buildings.

### The Pirate Plague

Between the 1560s and the 1680s Campeche was attacked again and again by pirates such as Henry Morgan and the Dutchman known simply as "Peg-Leg". Finally, the Spanish governors and city's merchants had enough and ordered the building of a solid ring of walls and bastions. Thus Campeche became one of the largest walled cities in Spanish America.

Left **Mayan writing** Center **Fort at Campeche** Right **Mexican revolutionary poster**

# Top 10 Moments in Yucatán History

### 1 2000 BC–AD 100: Early Cultures

The Maya emerge in the Yucatán perhaps as early as 2000 BC. But it is not until 300 BC–AD 100 that the distinctive characteristics of their culture appear – such as a writing system, calendar, and city states. For these attributes, the Maya owe much to the first great culture of Ancient Mexico, the Olmecs, who thrived between 1500 and 300 BC.

**Olmec carving**

### 2 250–900: Classic Era Mayan Civilization

For over 500 years in the Classic era, Mayan civilization flourishes throughout the Yucatán, Chiapas, northern Guatemala, and Belize. And, from about 650, the culture expands vigorously in the northern Yucatán, reaching its peak at Chichén Itzá and Uxmal.

### 3 800–950: Collapse of Mayan Civilization

In the relatively short span of about 150 years, Mayan civilization almost disappears, most likely due to a series of catastrophes – overpopulation, over-use of exhausted land, intensification of inter-Mayan wars, and drought. The southern city states are left deserted, and the Mayan writing system virtually disappears. In the north, the decline is later, and the cities are never entirely abandoned.

### 4 1150–1520: Post-classic Revival

After a 200-year gap, Mayan culture is revived on a modest scale in the northern Yucatán, with the city of Mayapán. Smaller cities, such as Tulum, Cozumel, and El Rey (Cancún), develop near the Yucatán coast and become important links in a trade route running between the Aztecs of Central Mexico and South America.

### 5 1517: Spaniards Arrive

An expedition led by Francisco Hernández de Córdoba sails from Cuba and makes the first Spanish landfall in Mexico on Isla Mujeres. It continues to Campeche and Champotón, then is attacked by the Maya and forced to turn back.

### 6 1526–42: Spanish Conquest

The Yucatán is conquered on the third attempt by conquistadores

**Painting of the Spanish Conquest**

led by three members of the Montejo family. Having been besieged for months in the ruins of ancient Ti'ho, they make this the site of their new city of Mérida.

7 **1821: Independence**
As Spain's American Empire collapses, the Yucatán, which has had its own administration under Spanish rule, grudgingly agrees to become part of an independent Mexico, but declares independence a few years later. In 1842 a Mexican attempt to reincorporate the Yucatán by force is beaten back.

8 **1847: Caste War Begins**
Mayans across the Yucatán rise against their white and *mestizo* (mixed-race) rulers in the best-organized Native American revolt anywhere in the Americas since the Conquest – and they almost succeed. The main Caste War is over by 1850, but rebels continue to defy Mexican authority until 1902 – some carry on until 1930.

9 **1860–1910: Henequen Boom**
The Yucatán's economy is transformed as global demand soars for sisal rope, made from the *henequen* cactus. This "green gold" is the best rope in the world until the arrival of synthetics in the 1950s. Vast new wealth is reflected in Mérida's extravagant mansions, theaters, and other attractions for *henequen* magnates and hacienda-owners. The boom even partly survives the Mexican Revolution, which begins in 1910.

10 **1971: Tourism Arrives**
Another economic transformation begins as the first hotel opens in Cancún, the dawn of the tourism era.

## Gods and Spirits of the Ancient Maya

1 **Itzamná**
Paramount god in the Postclassic Yucatán, the inventor of writing and the god of medicine.

2 **Ixchel**
The goddess of fertility, childbirth, and weaving.

3 **Maize God**
One of the foremost gods, created by the First Mother and First Father (maize was essential in ancient America).

4 **Hero Twins**
In Mayan myths, the twins Hunahpú and Xbalanqué have many adventures and defy the forces of death.

5 **Chac**
Mayan god of rain and lightning, identifiable in carvings by his long, curling snout.

6 **Tlaloc**
A Central Mexican god of rain and war, with strange, round "goggles" on his eyes.

7 **Kukulcán**
A powerful bird-serpent, the Central Mexican god Quetzalcoatl was known in the Yucatán as Kukulcán.

8 **Vision Serpents**
Conduits between men and the gods, they were summoned up by Mayan lords and shamans during rituals.

9 **Cosmic Turtle**
Another symbol of water and the earth. In the Mayan creation myth, the Maize God emerges through a crack in the shell of the cosmic turtle.

10 **Earth Lord**
The Maya viewed the earth as a living being, which could be kindly or monstrous. Monstermouth temples *(see p30)* are often representations of the Earth Lord.

Left **El Rey, Cancún** Right **Masks, Edzná**

# TOP 10 Popular Mayan Ruins

**Ball Court, Cobá**

### 1 Chichén Itzá

The most dramatic of the Mayan cities has gigantic buildings, including the great pyramid that has become a symbol of the Yucatán *(see pp22–5)*. *Map E3*

### 2 Tulum

A small city from the last decades of Mayan civilization, Tulum is spectacular as the only Mayan city built above a beach *(see pp18–19)*. *Map G4*

### 3 Cobá

The largest and most powerful city in northern Yucatán before the rise of Chichén Itzá. Buildings are spread over a huge area of dense forest and lakes (bikes can be rented). The Nohoch Mul, at 42 m (138 ft), is the highest pyramid in the Yucatán *(see p89)*. *Map F3*

### 4 Ek-Balam

This compact city was little known until recently. Excavations of its largest temple-mound in 1998 revealed spectacular carvings, especially at El Trono ("The Throne"), the largest and most extravagant of Mayan monstermouth temples. Other unique buildings include an almost spiral-shaped tower, La Redonda, the design of which is a mystery *(see also p98)*. *Map F2*

### 5 Dzibilchaltún

Just north of Mérida, this site was occupied for over 2,000 years. At dawn on spring and summer equinoxes, the sun strikes straight through the open doorways of the Temple of the Seven Dolls and along a road. There's also a great swimming cenote here *(see pp53 & 105)*. *Map C2*

**The three-story, 90-room palace at Sayil**

Temple of the Seven Dolls, Dzibilchaltún

### 6 Uxmal

A hugely atmospheric city with some of the finest Mayan buildings, in the Nunnery Quadrangle and the Governor's Palace *(see pp28–31)*. *Map C4*

### 7 Kabah

Second in importance among the Puuc cities *(see p31)* after Uxmal, to which it was linked by a *sacbé* or Mayan road. A grand arch over the end of this path forms a pair with the arch at Uxmal *(see p29)*. The great highlight is the Codz-Poop or "Palace of Masks," with a façade that has over 250 long-nosed Chac faces *(see also p106)*. *Map C4*

### 8 Sayil

Among the wealthiest of the Puuc towns, with around 17,000 inhabitants in AD 850. Its magnificent Palacio has been likened to ancient Greek buildings. The Mirador pyramid was the center of the town's market area *(see also p106)*. *Map C4*

### 9 Labná

One of the most beautiful of all Mayan sites, in a wooded valley full of colorful birds. Walking around it gives a strong impression of the life that went on here. Though small, it has fine buildings, above all the Arch of Labná *(see p106)*. *Map C4*

### 10 Edzná

Another of the largest and wealthiest cities of Classic-era Yucatán *(see p36)*. Its huge palace, the "Building of the Five Stories", is the largest and most complex of all Mayan multistory buildings *(see also p35)*. *Map B5*

## Top 10 Quieter Ruins

**1 El Rey, Cancún**
The relics of the historic occupiers of Cancún Island *(see p9)* .

**2 El Meco, Cancún**
The most important city near Cancún in pre-Hispanic times *(see p78)*.

**3 San Gervasio, Cozumel**
Capital of the island when it was one of the great pilgrimage centers of Mayan Yucatán *(see pp10–11)*.

**4 Xel-Ha**
One of the oldest Mayan sites near the modern Riviera, with ancient murals of birds *(see also p19)*.

**5 Muyil**
A very old Mayan site next to the Sian Ka'an reserve, with several pyramids amid the forest *(see p21)*.

**6 Aké**
Built of massive columns and huge stone slabs, this city is unlike anywhere else in the Yucatán, making it a challenge to archeologists. *Map C2*

**7 Xcambó**
A tiny site, probably an offshoot of Dzibilchaltún, with a Catholic chapel built onto one of its pyramids. *Map C2*

**8 Oxkintok**
Ancient city just west of the Puuc area. It rivalled Uxmal in size, and has a bizarre temple-labyrinth. *Map B3*

**9 Xlapak**
Smallest of the Puuc sites. Its Palacio has a frieze of elaborately carved Chac-masks. *Map C4*

**10 Mayapán**
The last major Mayan city, which dominated the Yucatán from 1200–1450, has striking painted frescoes. *Map C3*

Left **Church at Ticul** Center **Portico, Mérida** Right **Tiled icon at Santa Lucia, Mérida**

# TOP 10 Colonial Towns

### 1 Valladolid

Valladolid combines distinguished colonial architecture with the easygoing atmosphere of a Yucatán market town. Whitewashed arcades and 17th-century houses surround the main plaza, and among the town's many churches is a fine Franciscan monastery *(see p42)*. Right in the middle of the town is a huge cenote, which once provided all Valladolid's water, and nearby at Dzitnup *(see p52)* are some of the Yucatán's most spectacular cenotes for swimming *(see also p97)*.

### 2 Tizimín

The name comes from the Mayan *tsimin*, a kind of demon, which was also used to describe the Spaniards when they first appeared on horseback. Today it's the capital of Yucatán's "cattle country," between Valladolid and Río Lagartos. The pleasant twin plazas in the center are divided by two huge monasteries, which give Tizimín a distinctly Mediterranean appearance *(see also p100–101)*.

**Statue, Valladolid**

### 3 Izamal

Known as La Ciudad Dorada, the Golden City, because of the ocher wash of its buildings, this is the most complete and unchanging of Yucatán colonial towns. At its heart is the largest of the Yucatán's Franciscan monasteries *(see p43)*, and a short distance from this are the glowering pyramids of a much older Mayan city. Horse-drawn carriages, *victorias*, are a favorite way of getting around *(see also p99)*.

### 4 Mérida

The Yucatán's capital, founded by the Spaniards in 1542 on the site of the Mayan city of Ti'ho, has a seductive appeal. Whitewashed Spanish houses with shaded patios provide delightful places to stay. Despite the bustle of its market (and traffic), amid the city's old squares life still proceeds at a leisurely, friendly pace *(see pp26–7)*.

**Izamal**

### 5 Acanceh

An extraordinary little town in which over 2,000

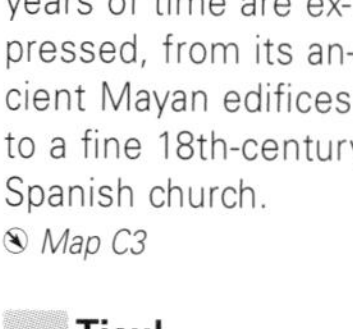

years of time are expressed, from its ancient Mayan edifices to a fine 18th-century Spanish church. ✎ *Map C3*

Colonial house doorway, Campeche

### 6 Ticul

The epitome of the slow-moving, unfussy, friendly atmosphere of a small Yucatán country town, Ticul also makes an excellent base for visiting the Puuc ruins *(see p31)*. Shoes are the town's traditional product, and it also has the Almendros Restaurant, credited with presenting Yucatán country cooking to the outside world *(see p71)*.

### 7 Oxcutzcab

The south of Yucatán near the Puuc hills is a fertile, fruit-producing region. Oxcutzcab has a huge market, where Mayan women in *huípiles* (white dresses with bright embroidery) preside over stalls stacked with succulent mangoes, papaya, oranges, watermelons, and more. Above them is the lofty tower of the town church, finished in 1645. ✎ *Map C4*

### 8 Maní

Now wonderfully sleepy, this town was important at the time of the Spanish Conquest, and contains the oldest Franciscan missionary monastery in the Yucatán, the scene of dramatic events in 1562 *(see p43)*. The town was the seat of Tutul Xiu, the first of the Mayan lords to accept Spanish authority in 1542. The monastery and town square occupy the top of an old Mayan temple-platform. ✎ *Map C4*

### 9 Teabo

With an air of tranquility, this remote town clusters around its grand and lofty Franciscan church, built in 1650–95. In the sacristy are rare murals of saints, discovered by accident in the 1980s. Teabo is also known for its fine embroidery. ✎ *Map C4*

### 10 Campeche

The most complete Spanish walled city in Mexico, Campeche is full of reminders of the era when it was a trading hub of Spain's empire and looked upon with greed by Caribbean pirates. In recent years the old city – with its churches, patios, Andalusian-style grill windows, and façades in delicate pastel colors – has been restored to refresh its distinctive charm *(see pp34–5)*.

18th-century church, Acanceh

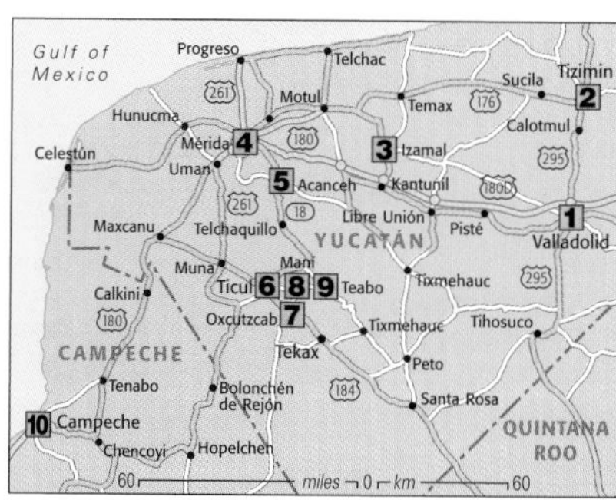

Left **Iglesia de Jésus** Center **Mérida Cathedral** Right **Las Monjas**

# Top 10 Churches

**San Bernardino Sisal, Valladolid**

### 1 San Bernardino Sisal, Valladolid

The oldest permanent church in the Yucatán began as part of a Franciscan monastery in 1552. It was located outside Valladolid so as to function both as a place of worship for the Spanish townsfolk and as a mission for Mayan villagers. Inside is a spectacularly painted Baroque altarpiece. The cloister surrounds an overgrown, palm-filled garden with a massive stone well from 1613, built over a natural cenote *(see also p97)*. ✎ *Map E3*

### 2 San Antonio de Padua, Izamal

The vast monastery of Izamal, painted ocher and white like the rest of the town *(see p40)*, epitomizes the plain, austere style favored by the Franciscan friars who brought Catholicism to the Yucatán. Founded in 1549, its huge *atrio*, or courtyard, was designed to hold great crowds of Mayans in open-air Masses. ✎ *Map D2*

### 3 Mérida Cathedral

The first cathedral completed in mainland America was built by local conquistadores in a style that the church leaders considered far too extravagant. The design is, in fact, quite simple, with few decorative flourishes, and the church's soaring white stone interior has great solemnity. The figures that you pass on the way in, flanking the imposing main entrance, represent saints Peter and Paul *(see also p26)*. ✎ *Map C2*

### 4 Iglesia de Jesús, Mérida

Built for the Jesuit Order and completed in 1618, the Jesús has a gilded Baroque interior that contrasts strikingly with the simplicity of the Franciscan churches. On the exterior, look out for traces of carvings on some of the stones – they were taken from Mayan temples *(see also p27)*. ✎ *Map C2*

**Doorway, La Mejorada**

### 5 La Mejorada, Mérida

This large church with a very Spanish-looking plain façade was built as part of a major Franciscan friary in 1640. It was the last



***Note:** Most churches are open around 7am–1pm and 4–9pm daily, but times can vary with little warning. Nearly all are free.*

occupied monastery in Mérida, and closed only in 1857. Behind the church, some of the former monastery buildings now house a school of architecture. ✎ *Map C2*

**Altar detail, Maní Monastery**

### 6 Las Monjas, Mérida

The church of "The Nuns" was built in the 1590s as a chapel for one of the first closed convents in the Americas. The castle-like mirador, or watchtower, with its unusual loggia (covered balcony) was built so that the nuns could take the air without leaving the convent. Sombre metal grills inside the church recall the separation that was kept between nuns and lay worshippers. ✎ *Map C2*

### 7 Maní Monastery

The first of all the Franciscan missionary monasteries in the Yucatán, consecrated in 1549, was built very simply, with a massive stone façade and cavernous cloister. Set within the façade was an external altar or "Indian Chapel," so that open-air services could be held in the square. In 1562, after the Franciscans discovered that many Mayans were practising their old religion in secret, an *auto da fé* was held in the square, during which the friars burned hundreds of Mayan manuscripts and pagan relics *(see also p41)*. ✎ *Map C4*

### 8 Tekax

Completed in 1692, this huge yet finely proportioned church was built in a lighter style than those of the early Colonial period. The churches at Teabo and Oxcutzcab are similar *(see p41)*. ✎ *Map C4*

### 9 Campeche Cathedral

Mérida and Campeche began their cathedrals around the same time, but the stop-start construction at Campeche meant that while the central façade was finished in the 1600s, the tower on its left was added only in the 1750s, and that on its right as late as the 1850s. ✎ *Map A5*

### 10 San Roque, Campeche

Campeche's churches are generally more colorful than those of Mérida and central Yucatán. San Roque is an extravagant example of Mexican Baroque, with an opulent altarpiece surrounded by intricate white plasterwork. ✎ *Map A5*

**Campeche Cathedral**

Left **Tulum** Right **Puerto Morelos**

# TOP 10 Beaches

**Cancún**

### 1 Cancún

This resort has the longest stretch of beach, backed by the biggest hotels and malls, and with the most attractions, from parasailing to water parks. The beaches on the north side of the island are the best for swimming and beach-life, but can get rather crowded. On the surf beaches along the east it is always possible to find a spot to yourself (but check safety conditions, *see p119*). *(See also pp8–9.)*

### 2 Isla Mujeres

Isla's small size means it has a more laid-back beach scene, especially on Playa Norte by Isla town, with its placid, safe waters. The island is a good-value diving center *(see also pp16–17)*.

### 3 Puerto Morelos

Despite its location between Cancún and Playa del Carmen, Puerto Morelos has avoided big-scale development. There's plenty of space along the long, white beach, where pelicans hang in the wind. A great snorkeling reef *(see p46)* lies close to the shore *(see also p76)*.

### 4 Playa del Carmen

The hippest and fastest-growing spot on the Mayan Riviera, with good shopping, strolling, bar-hanging, and people-watching opportunities in town, and miles of wonderful palm-lined bays stretching away to the north. To the south, the Playacar development has its own, narrower beaches *(see also pp12–13)*.

Left **Playa Norte, Isla Mujeres** Right **Playa Tukan, Playa del Carmen**

## 5 Cozumel

The island's fan base is split into three: divers, cruise passengers, and families. The finest diving locations are in the distant reefs, but the tranquil beaches along Cozumel's west coast are wonderful for a first experience of snorkeling. San Miguel town has a touristy but easygoing feel *(see also pp10–11)*.

## 6 Puerto Aventuras

This Mediterranean-style resort town was purpose-built from scratch around a natural inlet in the coast. It now contains the Riviera's best-equipped yachting marina, surrounded by a smart holiday village of villas and condo apartments. There's also a Dolphin Discovery Center *(see p17)*, a golf course, tennis center, and several big hotels.

## 7 Akumal

A lovely area that extends through beautiful, sweeping bays of white sands and gentle seas. Some big hotels have opened, but along most of the bays are secluded condo apartments and villas. It's an excellent diving center *(see also pp47 & 88)*.

## 8 Tulum

The favored place in the Yucatán for anyone wanting to settle into a palm-roofed cabin by a beach for a while. Head to the north end for cheap cabins where you get to know your neighbors, or turn south for more seclusion and seductive comforts in some cabins *(see also pp18–19 & 47)*.

**Akumal**

## 9 Progreso

Every weekend and in July and August thousands of Meridanos head up the road to Progreso, to lie on the beach and eat in its many great seafood restaurants. The atmosphere is bustling, friendly, and very Mexican. The opal-colored sea is ideal for swimming *(see also p105)*.

## 10 Celestún

Most tourists go to Celestún only to see its flamingos *(see p49)*, but it is also a tranquil village with an endless white-sand beach lined by fishing boats. There are some very enjoyable beach restaurants *(see p111)* and often wonderful sunsets over the Gulf of Mexico *(see also p105)*.

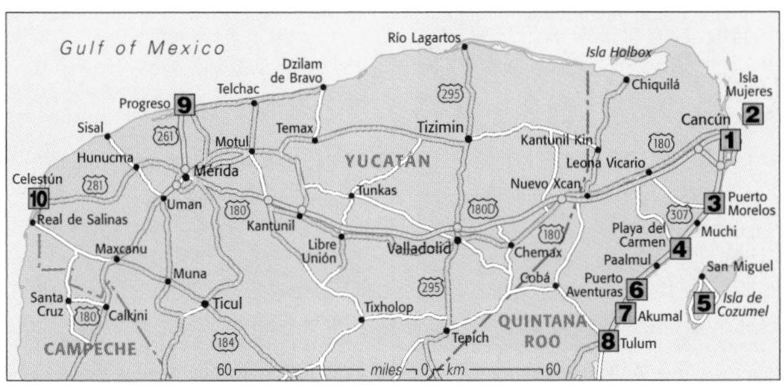

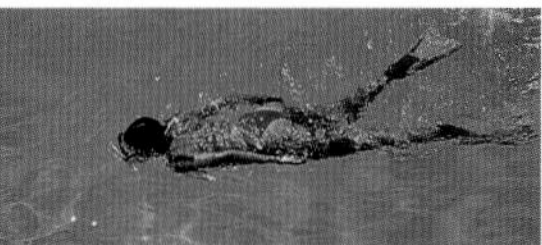

Left **Paradise Reef** Right **Snorkeling**

# TOP 10 Diving Reefs

### 1 Reefs around Cancún

Despite busy beaches and the relatively small size of the closest reefs, there's still lots to see here. "Jungle" snorkeling tours take you through mangroves in Laguna Nichupté and to the reef off Punta Nizuc *(see also pp8–9)*. *Map K4 & K6*

### 2 Manchones, Isla Mujeres

A fascinatingly varied reef, 1 km (half a mile) long, but only 10 m (30 ft) deep for much of it. The Sac Bajo area, just off the lagoon south of Isla Town, is excellent for snorkeling, and there are spectacular reefs farther from the island *(see also pp16–17)*. *Map L2*

**Fish swimming amongst the coral**

### 3 Paraíso, Cozumel

Cozumel offers the greatest extent and variety of reefs for snorkelers and divers of every level of experience, and visibility is ideal. Paraíso and nearby Chankanaab are "must-sees", with parrot fish, silver shoals of snappers and strangely shaped coral just below the surface *(see also pp10–11)*. *Map R5*

### 4 Palancar, Cozumel

An extraordinary coral mountain riven with giant canyons that seem to fall straight from the surface to the invisible depths of the ocean. Nearby, the Yucab and El Cedral reefs are also famous for their colonies of moray eels and groupers, and tree-like coral heads *(see also pp10–11)*. *Map Q6*

### 5 Puerto Morelos

One of the most vibrant of the mainland beaches and now officially protected as a *parque maritimo*. The reef is unusually close to the shore, and so is great for snorkel tours and introductory diving. The few dive and snorkel operators in Puerto Morelos give personal, friendly service *(see also p76)*. *Map R3*

### 6 Playa del Carmen and Chunzubul

Playa is the base for several very high-standard dive operators, who take beginners' groups and experienced divers to the reefs nearby and elsewhere along the Riviera *(see also pp12–13)*. *Map Q4*



*For a list of dive centers in the Yucatán* **see p124**

Turtle

## 7 Xpu-Ha

The superb reefs offshore here are a favorite destination for Playa del Carmen dive operators. Angelfish, triggerfish and parrot fish are abundant, along with a luxuriant range of coral *(see also pp86–9)*. ✎ *Map P5*

## 8 Akumal

The beaches here are an important breeding area for sea turtles, which coexist with the development along the bays. The reefs fringing the beaches are wonderful for snorkeling and diving *(see also p88)*. Akumal is also an important cave-diving center, with the Villas de Rosa Hotel *(see p130)*. ✎ *Map P5*

## 9 Tankah

A less well-known beach with just a few hotels *(see p130)* that's great for relaxed snorkeling and diving away from the crowds. As at Akumal, the reef comes quite close to the shore *(see also p90)*. ✎ *Map P6*

## 10 Tulum

This is the Riviera's biggest center for cave-diving *(see pp52–3)*, but dive operators also take snorkelers and divers to the reefs nearby, in a deliciously clear sea *(see also pp18–19)*. ✎ *Map P6*

## Top 10 Reef Animals

**1 Fan Corals**
Delicately veined fronds coming up from the ocean floor, which wave graciously in the undersea currents.

**2 Sea Cucumbers**
Tube-like creatures with a tough, spiny skin that can be seen lying motionless on the seabed or in clefts in the coral.

**3 Snappers**
Among the commonest fish here, yellowtail, blackfin, and other snappers move in huge, gleaming shoals.

**4 Angelfish**
Spectacularly colorful fish, with a fan-like shape and luminous stripes and patches in yellows and electric blue.

**5 Sergeant Majors**
Bright, darting, little fish, recognizable by their black and yellow vertical stripes.

**6 Pufferfish**
Bizarre fish that, when provoked, inflate themselves by taking in water in order to deter attackers.

**7 Parrot Fish**
These come in many varieties and sizes, but most are very colorful and look as if they are smiling amiably.

**8 Rays**
Spotted eagle rays, elegantly waving their "wings" as if to fly through the water, are common around some of the Cozumel reefs.

**9 Barracudas and Sharks**
Many varieties are found around the Yucatán reefs – but attacks on humans are almost unknown.

**10 Turtles**
Now endangered, sea turtles come ashore to lay their eggs on sandy beaches along the southern Riviera.

Left **Coral reef** Center left **Sea life from Rio Lagartos** Center right **Turtles** Right **Stork**

# TOP 10 Wildlife Reserves

### 1 Isla Contoy

This uninhabited island reserve north of Isla Mujeres is home to a huge range of sea birds, including pelicans, boobies, and frigate birds, and contains mangroves, turtle-breeding beaches, and superb coral lagoons. One-day tours are run by many dive shops and agencies from Isla and Cancún; check what your tour includes *(see also p17)*. *Map H1*

**Isla Contoy Pelican**

### 2 Parque Punta Sur, Cozumel

A very large area across the southern tip of Cozumel with an impressive variety of landscapes – forest, dunes, turtle beaches, snorkeling reefs, and tranquil mangrove lagoons – plus crocodiles, flamingos, and countless other birds. There are observation towers, an information center, and a maritime museum, and you can climb the Punta Celaraín lighthouse *(see also p11)*. *Map R6*

### 3 Puerto Morelos

The reef off Puerto Morelos is one of the least disturbed sections of coral near the mainland in the northern part of the Maya reef and is now protected as a marine park. Snorkelers can see spectacular marine life – lobsters, giant sponges, luminous parrot fish, and angelfish. Dive operators in the town offer low-impact snorkel and diving tours *(see also p46)*. *Map R3*

### 4 Sian Ka'an

Biggest by far of the Yucatán's nature reserves, this vast expanse of empty forest, mangroves, and lagoons gives an extraordinary glimpse of nature almost untouched by human habitation, and in all its complexity. Tulum is the starting point for trips into the reserve *(see pp20–21)*. *Map F6*

### 5 Punta Laguna

Spider monkeys are quite common in the Yucatán but often hard to see. Set in very dense forest around a lake near Cobá, this small village-run reserve is one of the places to find them. Villagers will guide you to the best spots, and monkeys are most likely to be around in the early morning and early afternoon *(see also p90)*. *Map N4 • daily*

**Punta Sur**



*For information on eco and adventure tours* **see p124**

Uaymitún

## 6 Río Lagartos

A huge, long, narrow lagoon of creeks, mangroves, and mud- and salt-flats along the north coast of Yucatán that is tinged pink with colonies of 20,000 flamingos in the peak August breeding season. Fascinating, great-value boat trips are run from Río Lagartos and nearby San Felipe *(see also pp55 & 98).* *Map F1*

## 7 Bocas de Dzilam

Much more remote, this giant expanse of uninhabited mangrove lagoons extends west of San Felipe and also contains flamingo colonies and a variety of birds and other undisturbed wildlife. Getting there, with a boat trip over open sea, is a real adventure. *Map D1 • Boatmen in Río Lagartos, San Felipe, and Dzilam Bravo can be hired to take you to the mangrove lagoons • Trips last a full day*

## 8 Uaymitún

For easy bird-watching in the lagoons along the northern Yucatán coast, there is this free viewing tower, by the coast road east of Progreso, where even binoculars are provided. The top offers spectacular views over the wetlands to the south, and you can see flamingos, ducks, egrets, and, in winter, endless migratory birds from North America. *Map C2 • Free; donations appreciated*

## 9 Celestún

The most famous flamingo colonies in the Yucatán are in the lagoon beside this little town on the west coast. Launches run from a visitor center toward the pink streaks of flamingos on the horizon, passing fishermen's huts, ibises, and many other birds – an ornithologist's delight *(see also pp55 & 105).* *Map A2*

## 10 Campeche Petenes

The north of Campeche State behind the coast consists of mangrove lagoons and *petenes* – "islands" of solid land within the swamp, which have special microclimates all of their own. Within the area are flamingos, deer, and even pumas. Visitor facilities are very limited. *Map A4 • Boats can be hired in the village of Isla Arena, and tours are offered in Campeche*

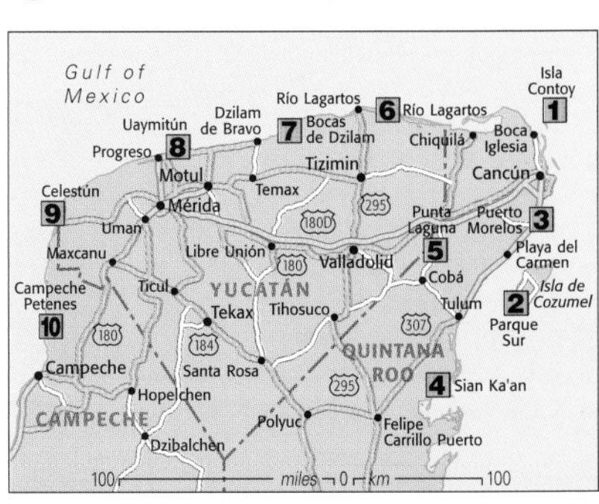

Left **Puma, Xcaret eco-park** Center **Dolphin Discovery** Right **Parque Garrafón**

# Top 10 Eco-Parks and Theme Parks

**Aqua World**

### 1 Aqua World, Cancún

A multi-activity fun center on Cancún Island offering jungle tours, submarine rides, jetskiing, snorkeling, diving, fishing, parasailing, dinner cruises, and tours to Isla Mujeres and Cozumel. *Blvd Kukulcán, km 15.2 • Map K5 • (998) 848 8300 • www.aquaworld.com.mx • 7am–3pm daily • Charges per activity*

### 2 Parque Nizuc, Cancún

The biggest water-fun park in Cancún has an interactive dolphin pool, a snorkeling pool with rays and innocent sharks, and a bungee-jump. But the biggest highlight is the Wet'n'Wild water park, with slides, rides, and wave pools for all ages *(see also p78)*. *Blvd Kukulcán, km 25 • Map J6 • (998) 193 2000 • www.parquenizuc.com • 10am–5pm daily • Adm*

### 3 Dolphin Discovery

There are three of these sea enclosures – on Isla Mujeres, at Chankanaab on Cozumel, and at Puerto Aventuras. At Cozumel you can swim or dive with the dolphins, ride on them, or be pushed along in the "footpush". *Map L1 • (998) 849 4757 • www.dolphindiscovery.com • Programs at 10am, noon, 2pm & 4pm daily • Adm • Min age 8 • Reservations essential*

### 4 Parque Garrafón, Isla Mujeres

A broad, natural pool of rock and coral is the central attraction. There's also a swimming pool, and snorkeling reefs just offshore. Good for novices. *Map L2 • (998) 877 1100 • www.garrafon.com • Summer: 8:30am–6:30pm (to 5pm in winter) • Adm*

### 5 Tres Ríos

Thick forest, cenotes, jungle streams, mangrove lagoons, beaches, and reefs are all found within this big eco-park north of Playa del Carmen. Bikes and kayaks are included in the ticket; optional extras include horse riding, snorkeling, reef-runner

**Parque Nizuc**

tours, scuba diving, a kids' club, paintball, and a blindfolded walk that allows you to experience the forest through touch and smell *(see pp76–7)*. *Map R4 • (998) 887 8077 • www.tres-rios.com • 9am–5pm daily • Adm*

**Xcaret eco-park**

## 6 Xcaret

The Riviera's original eco-park provides a spectacular introduction to the richness and variety of a tropical environment, all in one space *(see pp14–15)*.

## 7 Laguna Chankanaab, Cozumel

A great place to see Cozumel's undersea treasures with an easy swim, this small nature and snorkeling park lies close to the Chankanaab and Paraíso reefs *(see p46)* and includes a beach, a botanical garden, and a Dolphin Discovery center *(see entry 3)*. *Map R5 • 8am–6pm daily • Adm*

## 8 Aktun-Chen

From the highway near Akumal, a dirt track leads west through thick bromeliad-filled jungle to a nature park set around a vast cave and cenote system. You can't swim in the cenote, but the guided tours through the stalactite-filled cavern are highly impressive. Colorful birds, monkeys, and wild boars can be seen outside. *Map P5 • (998) 892 0662 • www.aktunchen.com • 9am–5pm daily (to 6pm Jun–Aug) • Adm*

## 9 Xel-Ha

One of the Riviera's most popular attractions, this snorkel park was created around a magnificent natural coastal lagoon that's especially good for children. It can seem crowded, but if you swim a bit away from the landing stages, you'll still find plenty of fish and coral. There are also forest trails to explore *(see also p88)*. *Map P6 • (998) 883 0524 • www.xelha.com.mx • 9am–6pm daily • Adm*

## 10 Dos Ojos Cenote and Hidden Worlds

The upper chambers of the world's longest underwater cave system, the Dos Ojos Cenote, are used by the Hidden Worlds center for one of the Yucatán's most exciting tours. After a hike during which a guide points out features of the forest, visitors can snorkel or scuba dive through crystal-clear cave waters in giant arched-roof caverns *(see also p19)*. *Map P6 • (984) 877 8535 • www.hiddenworlds.com.mx • Tours at 9am, 11am, 1pm daily • Adm*

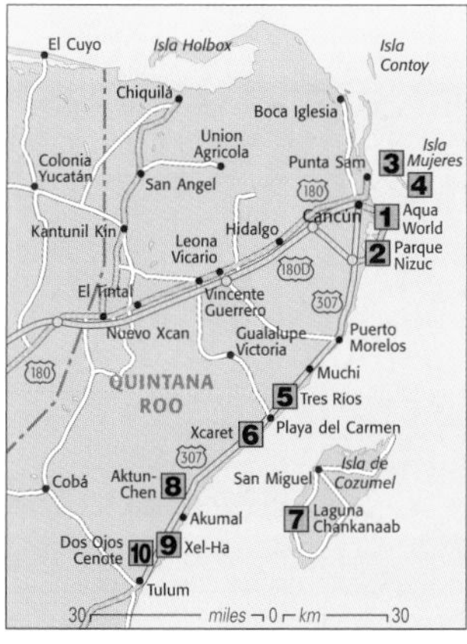

Left **Cenote Kantun-Chi** Center **Samula** Right **Dos Ojos**

# TOP 10 Cenotes and Caves

### 1 Cenote Kantun-Chi

There are several cenotes on the landward side of the highway near Xpu-Ha that can be easily accessed by visitors. A broad, shady pool dappled by brilliant sunlight, Kantun-Chi is near the road but refreshing for swimming. Neighboring cenotes Cristalino and Azul are also beautiful. *Map P5 • www.kantunchi.com • 9am–5pm daily • Adm*

### 2 Dos Ojos Cenote

This cavern is called "Two Eyes" because its two entrances look like eyes when seen from above. Extending over 60 km (37 miles) through a labyrinth of caverns and limestone "trees," it has been considered the world's longest underwater cave system – but the nearby Nohoch Nah Chich cenote may be even longer. Inexperienced divers get most from it with the Hidden Worlds tours *(see pp19 & 51)*. *Map P6*

**Cenote Dzitnup**

### 3 Gran Cenote

The loveliest of several cenotes open to swimmers along the road from Tulum to Cobá. Gran Cenote has a placid, clear pool, and snorkelers can make their way through a massive, arched cavern and down along a tunnel. *Map N6 • Sunrise–sunset daily • Adm*

### 4 Cenote Dzitnup

The most famous of the swimmable cenotes, a vast limestone cathedral. Via a narrow tunnel you enter a truly awe-inspiring chamber with a pool of perfect turquoise water at the bottom. Tour groups tend to visit about 11am–noon, but at other times it's rarely crowded *(see also p97)*. *Dzitnup village, 5 km (3 miles) W of Valladolid • Map E3 • 8am–5pm daily • Adm*

### 5 Cenote Samula

Another spectacular cavern-pool next to Cenote Dzitnup. Past a narrow entrance there's a huge pool of cool, clear water, and in the middle of the cave the roots of a giant ceiba tree – associated with mystical powers by the Maya – stretch straight down from the surface to reach the water far below. *Dzitnup village • Map E3 • 8am–5pm daily • Adm*

*Cenotes, sink-holes or water-filled caves in the limestone rock, are among the unmissable features of the Yucatán –* **see also p19**

Sacred Cenote, Chichén Itzá

### 6 Balankanché Caves

As well as cenote pools and underwater rivers, the Yucatán is underlain by a huge web of dry caves, sacred places to the ancient Maya. Balankanché, near Chichén Itzá, is one of the largest and most extraordinary cave systems *(see also p98)*. *Map E3 • Daily, guided tours only • Adm*

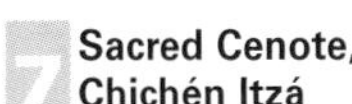

### 7 Sacred Cenote, Chichén Itzá

The most celebrated cenote in the Yucatán, the giant sacred well at Chichén *(see p23)*, has long been said to have been a place of human sacrifice. The cenote was used only for ritual purposes, perhaps as a channel to the Underworld, since the city's drinking water came from the Xtoloc Cenote, near the Caracol. *Map E3 • Adm as for Chichén Itzá*

### 8 Cenote Xlacah, Dzibilchaltún

The wide, round cenote that provided water for the ancient city of Dzibilchaltún is still a popular swimming hole today. It gets busy on Sundays but is a relaxing place for a dip at other times of the week *(see also p105)*. *Map C2 • 8am–5pm daily • Adm (Sun free)*

### 9 Calcehtok

These little-known caves near the Mayan ruins at Oxkintok *(see p108)* are some of the region's most extraordinary. The roofless main chamber is big enough to contain whole trees, and is full of birds. *Map B3*

### 10 Loltún Caves

An astonishing cave system not far from the Puuc cities *(see p31)*, with the longest history of human habitation in the Yucatán. Chambers are full of bizarre rock formations, strange airflows and relics of their Mayan occupants *(see also pp106–7)*. *Map C4 • Open daily; guided tours only • Adm*

Cenote Xlacah, Dzibilchaltún

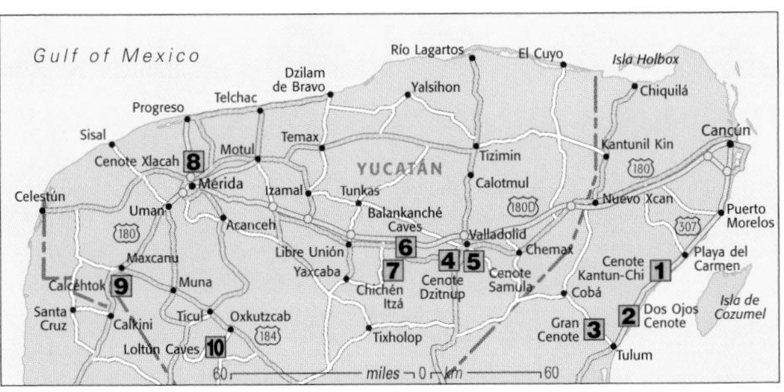

Left **El Paraiso, Tulum** Center **Holbox** Right **Río Lagartos**

# Top 10 Places To Get Away From It All

**Puerto Morelos**

## 1 Puerto Morelos

An undisturbed gem of the Mexican Caribbean, which has kept its mellow, fishing-village feel despite close proximity to Cancún. No real nightlife, but lovely beaches, and many small hotels and apartments offer long-term rates *(see also pp48 & 76).* *Map R3*

## 2 Punta Bete

A well-rutted track off the main Highway just north of Playa del Carmen leads in three bumpy kilometers (2 miles) to superb, curving beaches of dazzling white sand and a perfect turquoise sea. Some resort hotels have opened up here, but there are still clusters of laid-back beach *cabañas (see p126)* among the palms *(see also p76).* *Map R4*

## 3 Akumal

Not a remote spot, but the curving beaches here are very long and often occupied only by a few small-scale hotels and condo apartments. It's quite easy to find uncrowded space at Akumal, by an idyllic sea and with creature comforts included. There are also excellent diving facilities here *(see also p88).* *Map P5*

## 4 Tulum

The epitome of a tropical paradise: palm-shaded cabins only a few steps from a vividly colored sea, and with just candlelight and the sound of waves at night. The bargain *cabañas* at the north end of the beach are slightly noisier, so head south for pure tranquility *(see also pp18–19).* *Map P6*

## 5 Punta Allen

The atrocious state of the road keeps visitor numbers down, but the trek deep into Sian Ka'an (4-wheel-drive only) takes you to a tiny fishing village of sand streets and giant palms, with landing stages by the beach and a few easy-going restaurants and

**The bay at Punta Allen**

welcoming places to stay. Local guides offer snorkeling, bird-watching, and fishing trips *(see also p21)*. *Map G5*

### 6 Holbox

If the Riviera seems just too busy, take a long drive north from the Cancún–Mérida road to the tiny port of Chiquilá. Hop on a ferry to cross the beautiful lagoon (where dolphins are common) to reach the island of Holbox. Here you'll find the simple pleasures of a friendly village, a long, empty beach, and some very mellow places to stay *(see also p79)*. *Map G1*

### 7 El Cuyo

With just one hotel, two sets of beach *cabañas*, and a couple of places to eat – with great fresh fish – this Gulf-coast fishing village is for anyone who really does want a beach all to themselves *(see also p100)*. *Map F1*

### 8 Río Lagartos and San Felipe

Celebrated for the spectacular flocks of flamingos in the lagoon to their east *(see p49)*, these villages delight visitors with their unhurried, easy-going style. Great seafood restaurants too, as well as some pleasant small hotels, and, from San Felipe, wonderful sunsets *(see also pp49 & 98–9)*. *Map E–F1*

### 9 Celestún

Flamingos, again, are the big attraction here, but if you stay over in one of the small hotels after the day-trippers have returned to Mérida

Hacienda Katanchel, Mérida

you can sample a delightfully peaceful village, its beach strewn with fishing boats *(see also pp49 & 105)*. North of Celestún is a really remote beach retreat at Xixim *(see p126)*. *Map A2*

### 10 Hacienda Hotels

A seductive escape is offered (at upscale prices) by the hotels scattered around the Yucatán in beautifully converted old Colonial haciendas (country estates). All have luxurious rooms surrounded by tropical gardens, with superb pools and fine restaurants *(see also p127)*.

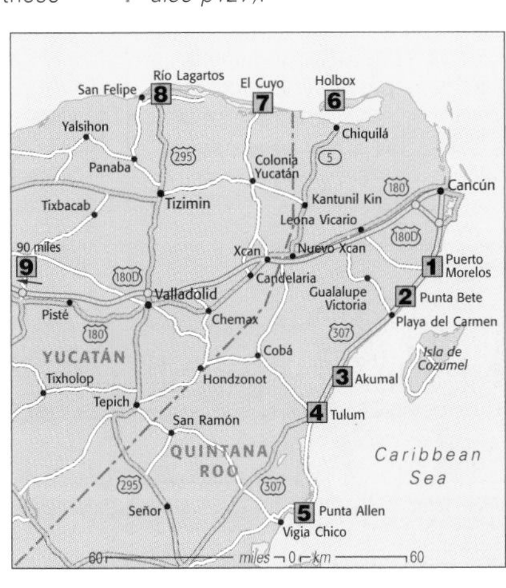

Left **Tennis in Cancún** Center **Dive shop, where sea-fishing trips can be arranged** Right **Cycling**

# Top 10 Sports and Activities

**Playacar Golf Club**

## 1 Golf

Golfers on the Riviera have a choice of two championship-level courses at Cancún, one in Playacar and one at Puerto Aventuras. Hotels can book greens for you. There is also a private club north of Mérida, which can be booked through hotels. ✆ *Club de Golf Cancún (998) 883 1230 • Palace Resort (01800) 672 5223 Extn. 2 • Puerto Aventuras Golf Club (984) 873 5109*

## 2 Fishing

Conditions for deep-sea and inshore fishing are outstanding, and the lagoons south of the Riviera by Ascension Bay are a must for fly-fishing fans. The peak deep-sea fishing season is March–June *(see box, right).*

## 3 Sailing, Windsurfing, and Kayaking

The best places to rent boats are Isla Mujeres and Cozumel. Hotels may have dinghies for guests. Windsurfing is at its finest around Isla Mujeres and Akumal, and the best kayaking is around Puerto Morelos, Punta Solimán *(see p91)*, or Tres Ríos *(see pp50–51)*. ✆ *Aquaworld (998) 848 8300*

## 4 Tennis

Many resort hotels have tennis courts. In Cancún, Hotel Omni's courts are open to all, while those at Hotel NH Krystal are for residents. The Club de Golf Cancún *(see entry 1)* has two courts. ✆ *Hotel NH Krystal (998) 848 9800 • Hotel Omni (998) 881 0600*

## 5 Cycling

The most attractive places to get around by bike are Cancún, Isla Mujeres, Tulum, and Valladolid, where there's a lovely cycle path to Cenote Dzitnup *(see p52)*. Many Cancún hotels have bikes, and there are rental shops in the other three destinations.

**Horse Riding, Cozumel**

*For information about diving and snorkeling,* **see pp46–7**

Touring a Mayan village

## 6 Horseback Riding

Take group treks at Rancho Loma Bonita, near Puerto Morelos, Rancho Buenavista on Cozumel, and at Tres Ríos and Xcaret *(see pp14–15, 50–51).*

*Rancho Loma Bonita (998) 887 5465 • Rancho Buenavista (987) 872 1537 Extn. 120*

## 7 Parasailing

Soar above Cancún with the "Skyrider" from Aqua World *(see p50).* More basic parasailing operations are found along Cancún beach and at Playa del Carmen.

## 8 Skydiving

Sky Dive Playa will give you the long-distance view of the Riviera as you plummet on the back of an instructor, or on your own if you have skydiving experience. *Sky Dive Playa (984) 873 0192 • www.skydive.com.mx*

## 9 Air Tours

Aerosaab, at Playa del Carmen, offers aerial sightseeing tours over the Riviera, Chichén Itzá, and other parts of the Yucatán Peninsula, for around $150 per person. *Aerosaab (984) 873 0804 • www.aerosaab.com*

## 10 Jungle Tours

Playa-based ATV Explorer lets you race through the woods on four-wheel ATVs (All-Terrain Vehicles). Alltournative offers group trips by truck, jeep, and kayak. *ATV Explorer (984) 873 1626 • Alltournative (984) 803 9999; free from USA and Canada (800) 507 1092 • www.altournative.com*

# Top 10 Fishing Locations

## 1 Cancún

For easy-access, fun fishing, with trips available from watersports centers like Aqua World *(see p50).*

## 2 Isla Mujeres

Highly regarded by deep-sea fishing enthusiasts, with able captains who seek out amberjack, marlin, and more.

## 3 Cozumel

A base for many expert deep-sea captains who also offer trips to the inshore flats.

## 4 Puerto Morelos

Much lower key than the islands, but deep water close to shore means superb fishing.

## 5 Playa del Carmen

Many Playa dive shops also arrange fishing trips, especially in the sailfishing season (Mar–Jun).

## 6 Puerto Aventuras

The most luxuriously equipped fishing center on the coast. Hosts a big deep-sea tournament each May.

## 7 Boca Paila and Punta Allen

Fly-fishing and above all bonefish followers make their way to the remote fishing lodges along this road.

## 8 Holbox

A long way from the convenience of the Riviera, but loved by fishermen who like a really relaxing time.

## 9 El Cuyo

The one bar, La Conchita, is the place to go to find a boat and a guide. Shark fishing is a specialty of the north coast.

## 10 Río Lagartos

No well-organized facilities, but boatmen here will show you their fishing grounds as well as the flamingo lagoons.

Left **Xcaret** Center Left **Xel-Ha** Center Right **Punta Laguna** Right **Iguana, Uxmal**

# Top 10 Attractions for Children

### 1 Parque Nizuc, Cancún

The number one fun center in the region. As well as the adrenaline-pumping rides that older kids love – the Wave Pool, Bubba Tub, and Twister – the Wet'n'Wild section also has a Kids' Park with gentler rides and slides for young children. The Baxal-Ha snorkeling pool, with rays and harmless sharks, is another big thrill for ages 8-plus.

*Parque Nizuc, Boulevard Kukulcán km 25 • Map J6 • (998) 881 3000 • www.parquenizuc.com • Summer: 10am–6pm daily (to 5pm in winter) • Adm*

Crococún

### 2 Crococún Crocodile Park

Kids meet crocs (over 300 of them) at this attractive small zoo of all-local wildlife. Multilingual guides give informative, entertaining tours, and it's well-organized, with opportunities to pet and feed baby crocodiles, deer, monkeys, parrots, and less familiar animals such as tepezcuintles (a kind of big rodent).

*Highway 307, km 30 • Map R3 • (998) 850 3719 • www.crococunzoo.com • Summer: 9am–6pm daily (to 5pm in winter) • Adm*

Parque Nizuc, Cancún

### 3 Tres Ríos

All the region's eco-parks *(see pp50–51)* are family-friendly, but Tres Ríos goes a bit further with a special Kids' Club, where parents can leave small children to play and join in group activities in the forest and park *(see also pp76–7)*.

*Map R4 • www.tres-rios.com • 9am–5pm daily • Adm*

### 4 Laguna Chankanaab, Cozumel

One of the most enjoyable and accessible places for even small children to be dazzled by a real new experience – a first introduction to snorkeling and the underwater treasures of the Cozumel reefs. The sea is very placid and there's coral and abundant sea life just off the beach. In the same park there's also a coral lagoon, a botanical garden, and a Dolphin Discovery center *(see p50)*.

*Map R5 • 6am–6pm daily • Adm*

### 5 Playa Mia, Cozumel

Cozumel's beach clubs offer all the fun of the sand and sea, plus restaurants and loungers in

Xel-Ha

the shade. Playa Mia has the best choice of things to do for older children – snorkeling, beach games, kayaks, banana boats – and has a Kids' Club for little ones. *Map R6 • dawn–dusk daily • Adm*

## 6 Xcaret

The first and most famous of the eco-parks provides lots for kids to enjoy, in an easy, family-centered environment. The snorkeling river and dolphin pool are the biggest hits, but children can also enjoy the zoo, butterfly garden, and forest paths *(see also pp14–15). Map Q4 • (998) 883 3143 • www.xcaret.com.mx • Summer: 9am–7pm daily, winter: 8:30am–6pm daily • Adm*

## 7 Laguna Yal-Ku, Akumal

This winding rock pool of brilliant turquoise water right at the north end of Akumal's Media Luna Bay is one of the natural coral inlets on the Riviera coast. Rarely crowded, it's delightful for swimming and snorkeling with young children, with coral and colorful fish that are easy to spot. *Map P5 • 8am–6pm daily • Adm*

## 8 Xel-Ha

This snorkel park is another of the Riviera's big family attractions. Few kids are not enchanted by swimming and snorkeling in the coral lagoon, and exploring its lush forest setting *(see also p88). Map P6 • (998) 884 9422 • www.xelha.com.mx • 9am–6pm daily • Adm*

## 9 Punta Laguna

Getting to see local wildlife in the natural habitat, rather than in zoos or nature parks, can take a lot of time and effort, but at this small reserve north of Cobá you can see spider monkeys jumping through the trees after just a little exciting exploration. Village guides lead the way – deer, wild boar, and lots of birds can likely be seen too *(see also pp48 & 90). Map N4 • daily*

## 10 Uxmal

Some kids love Mayan ruins; others don't. But one that most frequently scores a hit is Uxmal. Not only does it have lots of steps and temples for running around, but it is also home to huge numbers of iguanas, which sit stock still until surprised, then dart off with sudden alacrity. Some are as big as crocodiles, but they're all harmless, no matter how scary they may look *(see also pp28–31). Map C4*

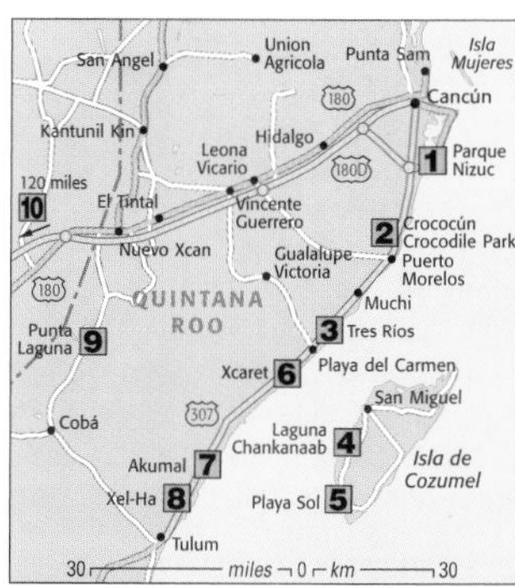

Left **Coco Bongo** Center **Hard Rock Café** Right **Carlos'n'Charlie's**

# Top 10 Nightspots

**1 Coco Bongo, Cancún**
The most state-of-the-art of them all among Cancún's mega-clubs, a vast, multilevel, multi-space venue with music that covers all the bases – techno, rock, Latin – from DJs and live bands, and a space to eat. Ultra-extravagant theme nights, live shows, and other eye-popping surprises are house specialties *(see p81)*. *Map L4*

**2 Dady'O, Cancún**
Always the most popular among American student "Springbreakers," this equally huge venue across the street from the Coco Bongo guarantees a noisy, down-home party atmosphere – theme parties are a permanent feature. Next door, the only slightly smaller Dady Rock is a live venue with a bar-restaurant, plus more fun and games *(see p81)*. *Map L4*

**3 Bulldog, Cancún**
If a Mexican band like Café Tacuba or Molotov is playing in Cancún, they are probably playing at the Bulldog. This nightspot is a little smaller than the other clubs in the neighborhood, but tables are set up in stadium-like tiers which ensures that there is no bad seat in the house. On non-show nights, DJs take over, usually playing to a mixed crowd of tourists and locals *(see p81)*. *Map L4*

**4 Dinner Cruises, Cancún**
For a slightly more sedate time try another Cancún specialty, with live shows, games, dinner, and dancing to live bands all on board as you sail around Laguna Nichupté or to Isla Mujeres. Each one is themed: Cancún Queen (from Aqua World,*(see p50)* is like an old stern-wheeled riverboat, the Columbus Lobster Dinner Cruise is on a replica Columbus-era galleon, and Captain Hook's Pirate Night is, of course, on a pirate ship *(see also p81)*.
*Columbus Cruise, Royal Mayan Marina, Blvd Kukulcán km 16.5 • Map K3 • (998) 848 8300*

**5 Blue Parrot, Playa del Carmen**
Playa del Carmen has changed enormously since its original beach bar opened in the early

**Blue Parrot**



**Note:** *In the big Cancún clubs, admission charges vary according to what's on – they're usually between $15 and $25*

La Santanera

1990s, but through it all the Parrot has remained the number-one place to meet up and mingle. There's always a buzzing scene, and you get a fabulous view of the moon over the sea *(see p81)*. ⊗ *Map Q4*

### 6 Diablito Cha Cha Cha, Playa del Carmen

At this stylish lounge, black and white floor tiles contrast with red and green furniture – an allusion to the colors in the Mexican flag. While you sip a vanilla martini and snack on Asian-style seafood the eclectic music ranges from rockabilly to electronica to homegrown pop *(see p82)*. ⊗ *Map Q4*

### 7 La Santanera, Playa del Carmen

Centrally located close to the main avenues in Playa del Carmen, this club features two separate levels playing different sounds (electronica downstairs, house music upstairs). It's a fun place for people of all ages, who come here to dance, drink, and enjoy the good ambience *(see also p81)*. ⊗ *Map Q4*

### 8 Hard Rock Café, Cozumel

The familiar burgers-and-rock'n'roll format found the world over is right by the waterfront in Cozumel. Live rock bands perform every night. There's also a big Hard Rock in Cancún, in the Forum by the Sea Mall *(see p82)*. ⊗ *Map R5*

### 9 Carlos 'n' Charlie's, Cozumel

Enjoyable, crowd-pleasing food and a non-stop, bright-and-breezy party atmosphere are the keys to the success of the Anderson group's bar-restaurants, found all around Mexico under several jokey names – Carlos'n'Charlie's, Sr. Frog's *(p82)*, and El Shrimp Bucket. The Cozumel C'n'C in Punta Langosta mall is one of the biggest *(see also p93)*. ⊗ *Map R5*

### 10 Pancho's, Mérida

Nightlife in Mérida is much more low-key than on the Riviera, but Pancho's, with its vaguely Mexican-bandit theme, is consistently the most enjoyable venue in the middle of town. Lively socializing is helped along by the fast and friendly staff, and at the back there's a dance floor under the stars *(see p110)*. ⊗ *Map C2*

Pancho's

Left **Teatro de Cancún** Right **Azúcar, Cancún**

# Top 10 Live Attractions

### 1 Mariachis, Cancún

High-quality mariachi bands perform traditional Mexican songs in many of the region's restaurants. This style of music dates back to the nineteenth century when Maximilian was emperor of Mexico. *La Parrilla, Av Yaxchilán 51 • Map K4 • (998) 884 5398 • OK. Maguey, Blvd Kukulcán km 13 local 173 • Map L4 • (998) 885 0503*

**Dancer, Teatro de Cancún**

### 2 Teatro de Cancún

This comfortable theater hosts two colorful, all-singing, all-dancing shows each weekday night: Voces y Danzas de México showcases Mexican traditional music and dance, while Tradición del Caribe is a more wide-ranging show with the rhythms of Cuba, Venezuela, Santo Domingo, and other spots around the Caribbean. *El Embarcadero, Blvd Kukulcán km 4.5 • Map K3 • (998) 849 4848 • Different shows are performed at different times throughout the night*

### 3 Azúcar, Cancún

Cancún's premiere Latin dance venue, where salsa fans can try out their slickest moves to top bands from Puerto Rico, Venezuela, Cuba, and around the Caribbean. It's a comfortable venue, and explosive, pulsating performances are guaranteed. *Punta Cancún, next to Hotel Dreams Cancún • Map L4 • (998) 848 7000 Extn. 7980 • From 9:30pm Mon–Sat*

### 4 Xcaret

The live show at the end of each day in Xcaret (included in the park ticket) presents many sides of Mexican traditions in colorful fashion, beginning with an impressive display of cowboy skills, going on to imagined versions of pre-Conquest Mayan rituals and dances, and ending with folk dances and music from around the country, from mariachis to the soft, dulcet tones of Yucatán boleros *(see also pp14–15)*. *Map Q4*

### 5 Bullfights

Full-scale Spanish-style bullfights take place starting the last Wednesday in December for 20 weeks in Cancún's bullring, preceded by a *charro* (cowboy) display – and sometimes cockfighting too. There's also a bullring in Mérida that's used less frequently, and bullfights feature in many Yucatán town fiestas *(see p64)*. *Plaza de Toros Cancún, corner of Av. Bonam-pak and Av. Sayil • Map J3 • (998) 884 8372 • Bullfights: 3:30pm Wed*

**Azúcar, Cancún**

Sound and light show, Chichén Itzá

### 6 Charrerías

A *charro* is a Mexican cowboy, in the famous outfit of big sombrero and embroidered jacket (*charras* are cowgirls, in similar hats but flounced skirts), and a *charrería* is a Mexican rodeo, a spectacular, competitive display of rope tricks, steer-wrestling, and astonishing horsemanship. There's no fixed *charrería* program in Cancún, but they come up fairly often. Mérida's *charro* ring has a similarly irregular schedule. *Rancho del Charro Cancún, Carretera del Aeropuerto km 4.5 • Map J4 • (998) 887 5963*

*Charrería* **(Mexican rodeo)**

### 7 Serenatas Yucatecas, Mérida

The very best introduction you can have to the Yucatán's distinctive music and folklore – the gentle, romantic music of guitar trios, the graceful *jarana* dance – is to go to one of these free concerts in the lovely setting of Mérida's Parque Santa Lucía. Held every Thursday for nearly 40 years, they are loved by locals still more than by tourists. *Map C2 • Performances: 9pm Thu*

### 8 Sound and Light Shows at Mayan Ruins

The great Mayan cities of Chichén Itzá and Uxmal are used as venues for daily shows in which their giant temples are dramatically lit in changing colors (included in the site ticket). Some parts of the commentary, "imagining" the cities' ancient history, are pretty far-fetched, but the visual effects are certainly spectacular *(see also pp22 & 29)*. *Map E3 & C4*

### 9 Serenatas Campechanas, Campeche

Campeche showcases its traditional music and dances with free concerts in the charming setting of the Colonial patio of the Casa Seis and, with a more eclectic program, from the bandstand of the Parque Principal *(see also p34)*. *Map A5 • Performances: Casa Seis, 8:30pm Thu*

### 10 Sound and Light Show, Campeche

The Puerta de Tierra, or "Land Gate," in the old city walls of Campeche provides the backdrop for a spectacular audio-visual show that uses the architecture well to evoke tales of pirates, sea battles, and other events in the city's maritime past *(see also p35)*. *Map A5 • Performances: 8pm Tue, Fri, Sat in winter; 8pm daily at Christmas, Easter, and summer*

Demonstration of Mayan ritual, Xcaret

Left **Mérida en Domingo** Right **Day of the Dead decoration**

# Top 10 Festivals

**Carnival celebrations in Mérida**

### 1 Carnival

The biggest and brightest celebration of the year in the cities of the Yucatán. In Cancún and Cozumel the streets fill with music, dancing, food stands, and a little Río-style parading. The biggest Carnival in southern Mexico, though, is in Mérida. *About one week before Lent*

### 2 Feast of Three Kings, Tizimín

The capital of Yucatán's cattle country hosts one of the region's biggest fiestas. It features a stock fair as well as bullfights, traditional music, dancing, colorful parades, and plenty of eating and drinking. *Map F2 • About two weeks from Jan 6*

### 3 La Candelaria

Valladolid's main fiesta, the Expo-Feria, centers around the Feast of the Virgin of La Candelaria. Local girls show off dazzling embroidered dresses in the opening parade, followed by free concerts and shows, and dancing. Campeche has a smaller celebration. *Map E3 • 12 days around Feb 2*

### 4 Equinoxes, Chichén Itzá and Dzibilchaltún

The visual effects integral to these Mayan cities – such as the "descent" of the sun down the serpents on El Castillo at Chichén and the striking of the rising sun through the Seven Dolls temple at Dzibilchaltún – were timed to happen on the spring and fall equinoxes. Today, over 80,000 people visit Chichén for the day; crowds are smaller at Dzibilchaltún *(see pp23 & 105)*. *Mar 21, Sep 21*

### 5 Mérida en Domingo

Mérida hosts a free fiesta every week, "Mérida on Sunday," when the Plaza Mayor and Calle 60 are closed to traffic to make way for strolling crowds and a range of events. There are displays of *jarana* dancing in front of the City Hall and concerts up and down the street, and anyone can dance, too. *Map C2 • Every Sun*

### 6 Village Fiestas

Every village and town in the Yucatán also has its own fiesta, when the streets are covered in bright garlands, work ceases, and music is heard non-stop. To find out when any are due, ask in tourist offices, look out for posters, or check local papers.

## 7 Cancún Jazz Festival

An innovative mix of young performers from Latin America, the U.S., and Europe – often playing Latin Jazz and contemporary fusion rather than strict jazz – features in this festival. Several acts play for free in Parque de las Palapas in Ciudad Cancún. *Three or four days, last weekend in May (U.S. Memorial Day weekend)*

## 8 San Miguel Arcángel, Cozumel

Cozumel's most important traditional fiesta is in honor of the island's patron saint, St. Michael. For nine days preceding his day, there are religious processions, kids' entertainment, and free music and dancing. *Sep 20–29*

## 9 Cristo de las Ampollas, Mérida

More solemnly religious than most fiestas, with processions culminating on October 13, when the figure of "Christ of the Blisters" (*Cristo de las Ampollas*), kept in Mérida Cathedral, is carried through the city before a ceremonial Mass. *Week before Oct 13*

## 10 Day of the Dead and All Saints' Day

Sugar skulls, dead bread (*pan de muerto*), zempazuchitl fowers, and coffin-shaped decorations are the mark of Mexico's most famous celebration, when people party to celebrate the dead on Halloween and All Saints' Day (*Todos Santos*), and families visit cemeteries to picnic by the graves of their own departed relatives. *Oct 31–Nov 2*

**Skull mask, Day of the Dead**

# Traditional Crafts and Products

## 1 Hammocks

The traditional place to sleep is so much a part of the Yucatán that local poets have even celebrated it in verse.

## 2 Embroidery

Lush flower designs are made by Mayan women on traditional *huípil* dresses, handkerchiefs, and tablecloths.

## 3 Panama Hats

The best palm hats are from northern Campeche; the place to buy them is Mérida.

## 4 Guayaberas

Light, elegant shirt-jackets, accepted as tropical formal wear, that give men (of a certain age) instant dignity.

## 5 Sandals

Huge racks of traditional leather *huarache* sandals can be found in all Yucatán markets.

## 6 Wood carving

Many Mayan villagers carve wooden figures based on ancient images.

## 7 Jícaras – Gourds

Dried natural gourd bowls, brightly painted, are a specialty of Chiapas, but are often seen in the Yucatán.

## 8 Silverwork and Jewelry

Fine silverware from Taxco in central Mexico is found in Yucatán stores, as well as amber from Chiapas.

## 9 Painted Birds and Ornaments

Brightly painted wooden parrots, toucans, and boxes provide one of the prettiest images of tropical Mexico.

## 10 Ceramics

Huge numbers of earthenware pots are made in Ticul, sometimes using pre-Conquest techniques.

Following pages **North Beach, Cancún**

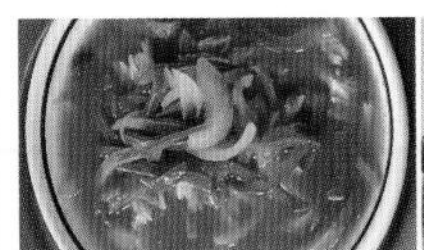

Left **Sopa de Lima** Center **Poc-Chuc** Right **Barbecued chicken stall**

# TOP 10 Dishes of the Yucatán

**1 Sopa de Lima**
One of the most popular classics of Yucatecan cooking, "lime soup" is actually made with chicken, boned, chopped in strips, and then slow-cooked with coriander, onions, herbs, spices, and masses of local sweet limes. It's then served with strips of dry tortillas for added crunch.

Cochinita Pibil

**2 Cochinita Pibil**
A dish that dates back to pre-Conquest Mayan cooking – pork marinated in lime, bitter orange, and *achiote* (a hot, spicy mix of dried herbs), wrapped in banana leaves and baked in an earthenware dish. Punchy but flavorful, it's very versatile and can be served as a main course or just used to make tacos. *Pollo pibil* is a chicken version of this dish.

**3 Poc-Chuc**
Marinating is one of the most characteristic skills of Yucatecan cooking, and this delicious dish features pork marinated in the juice of *naranja agria* (small, bitter oranges, special to the region), cooked with onions, herbs, and garlic and served with black beans. With a wonderful mix of sweet and savory flavors, it's very popular, but debate rages as to whether it is really traditional or a creation of Los Almendros restaurant in Ticul *(see p71)*.

**4 Pollo Oriental de Valladolid**
The special pride of Valladolid: chicken quartered on the bone and casseroled with garlic, onion, cloves, and a mix of both hot and mild chilis; it's then quickly roasted in a baste of maize oil and bitter orange juice. Another dish with a rich, densely layered combination of different flavors. *Pavo oriental* is the turkey version.

**5 Relleno Negro**
Yucatecan cooking likes rich concoctions. In *relleno negro* ("black stuffing"), finely ground pork, peppers, grated hard-boiled egg, herbs, spices, and a powerful combination of chilis are all mixed together to make up a thick, majestic sauce. Usually served with turkey *(pavo)*, the region's most traditional meat.

**6 Camarón al Mojo de Ajo**
All around the coasts, fish and seafood are restaurant staples. One of the simplest and most delicious ways of cooking the likes of *camarón* (prawns/shrimp) and *caracol* (conch) is *al mojo de ajo*, fried quickly in hot oil and loads of garlic. When ingredients are fresh, nothing more is needed.

**7 Crepas de Chaya**
Tasting rather like spinach, *Chaya* is a vegetable native to

*Yucatecan dishes are not always fiery, but you can pep them up with the red and green chili sauces that accompany most meals*

the Yucatán. And, like spinach, it is exceptionally rich in iron and vitamins. It features in traditional cooking and new dishes like this one, in which it is cooked with garlic and wrapped in light, soft European-style wheat pancakes (crêpes) and served with a cheese sauce. *Chaya* is also used to make drinks *(see p71)*.

8 **Pan de Cazón**
Campeche has a distinctive and very varied cuisine of its own that, as befits a port, makes great use of local fish and seafood. This is one of the most popular campechano favorites, and features chopped hammerhead shark *(cazón)*, mixed with spices and a tomato sauce; it is served between two soft corn tortillas.

9 **Arroz con Pulpo**
Another Campeche specialty: a delicious warm salad that's much lighter than many local dishes on a hot, hot day. Rice *(arroz)* is mixed together with chopped octopus *(pulpo)*, red peppers, onion, coriander, and other herbs, and often mango, papaya, and other fruits, in a refreshing blend of sweet juice and salty seafood flavors.

10 **Pollo con Mole**
Not a native of the Yucatán but a central Mexican classic that's found in every part of the country. Fried chicken covered in *mole*, a thick, spicy, savory – and not at all sweet – chocolate sauce. Richly satisfying, this is one of the oldest uses of chocolate, its flavor combining perfectly with strongly-spiced meats.

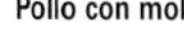

**Pollo con mole**

## Snacks

1 **Ceviche**
Raw fish or seafood marinated in lemon or lime juice, and served with salad, spices and lots of coriander.

2 **Cocteles**
Usually, fish or seafood ceviches served in a glass in a vinaigrette-style dressing.

3 **Papadzules**
A Mayan dish of chopped hard-boiled eggs in a sweet pumpkin-seed sauce, rolled in tortillas – often served with a spicy tomato sauce.

4 **Panuchos**
Small, crisp-fried tortillas covered in refried beans and topped with strips of chicken or turkey and chopped tomato, onion, avocado, and chilis.

5 **Salbutes**
Similar to *panuchos*, but made with a thicker, spongier base instead of crisp tortillas.

6 **Enchiladas**
In southern Mexico, these rolled soft tortillas with various fillings tend to be served with a rich *mole* sauce.

7 **Tacos**
Small rolled tortillas filled with 1,001 possible fillings: at taco stands, they're served rolled up; at *taquerías* you sit and assemble them yourself.

8 **Fajitas**
Pan-fried meat or seafood served sizzling with bowls of onions, refried beans, chili sauce, guacamole, and tortillas.

9 **Quesadillas**
Small, soft tortillas, folded over and filled with melted cheese and sometimes ham, served with various sauces.

10 **Tortas**
Small bread rolls, available with as many different fillings as tacos.

Left **La Habichuela** Center **Chen Río** Right **El Marlin Azul**

# Top 10 Restaurants

### 1 La Habichuela, Cancún

Excellent Yucatecan and Mexican cooking, with Campeche dishes such as *camarón al coco* (prawns/shrimp with coconut). Fine presentation and original touches, all superbly served in the tranquil surroundings of a lush garden *(see p83)*.

La Parrilla

### 2 La Parrilla, Cancún

At this colorful restaurant, Mexican art and music create an atmospheric background for the delicious local specialities on the menu, including Mayan dishes. Warm ambience, great food, and affordable prices have made La Parrilla a successful formula exported to other centers along the Riviera *(see p83)*.

### 3 Chen Río, Cozumel

With a fine beach all to itself, you can spend a leisurely afternoon here watching the waves and picking over the house specialty, a huge platter of mixed seafood, or sampling the excellent *ceviches* and salads *(see p95)*.

### 4 Los Pelícanos, Puerto Morelos

Set beneath a giant *palapa* palm roof, in a spot above the beach, this easygoing local institution serves some of the best *ceviches* you'll ever find, as well as grander seafood dishes *(see p83)*.

### 5 Kinich, Izamal

Tucked into a secluded garden near the largest of Izamal's Mayan pyramids, this is the place to sample the full range of Yucatecan cooking – *cochinita, pavo en relleno negro*, and a fragrant *sopa de lima* *(see p103)*.

### 6 El Marlin Azul, Mérida

It's easy to walk past this seafood restaurant and miss it. Look for a blue awning and a crowd of regulars perched at the counter – they're enjoying some of the best seafood in the city, trucked in daily direct from Celestún *(see p111)*.

### 7 Casa de Piedra, Xcanatún

Yucatecan and Caribbean traditions and ingredients are combined with sophisticated

Casa de Piedra

*For an explanation of the Yucatecan dishes,* **see pp68–9**

Los Almendros

international styles by a French-trained chef: a delicate *sopa de lima* is a menu fixture, alongside the chef's own interesting creations, such as cream of *poblano* chili soup with roquefort *(see p111)*.

### 8 John Gray's Place, Playa del Carmen

Chef John Gray first arrived in the Yucatán to open the Ritz-Carlton in Cancún. He decided to stay, and opened his own restaurant in Puerto Morelos. His second operation, in Playa del Carmen, is livelier but has the same simple, fresh food. Try the honey-glazed duck and chicken with cilantro pesto, which gained Gray his following. The drinks here are good too *(see p83)*.

### 9 Los Almendros, Ticul

This homey restaurant, which opened in the 1960s, is credited as the first to present Yucatecan cuisine to the outside world. Richly flavored dishes, charming service, and an essential part of a visit to the Puuc region *(see p111)*.

### 10 Marganzo, Campeche

The city's own fish and seafood specialties headline on the menu – juicy *pan de cazón*, and impressive platters of *manitas de cangrejo* (crab claws, served with a mix of other seafood, sauces, and salad) *(see p111)*.

## Breakfasts and Juices

### 1 Huevos Rancheros

A breakfast classic: tortillas topped by fried eggs, covered in spicy tomato sauce, and served with refried beans.

### 2 Huevos Motuleños

As above, but with the addition of peas, ham, and grated cheese – often served with slices of fried banana on the side.

### 3 Huevos Revueltos

Scrambled eggs, nearly always mixed with a little onion and red pepper, or with ham *(con jamón)*.

### 4 Huevos a la Mexicana

Spicy scrambled eggs – with peppers, chili, chopped onions, and chorizo sausage.

### 5 Chilaquiles

Crisp tortilla chips, baked in a cheese sauce with tomato, onions, herbs, chili, and shredded chicken or turkey.

### 6 Platillo de Fruta

A big plate of fresh fruit, usually including at least pineapple, watermelon, oranges, bananas, and papaya.

### 7 Agua de Jamaica

Enormously refreshing local product – an infusion of dried flowers of jamaica (a kind of hibiscus), diluted to make a delicious tall drink.

### 8 Agua de Chaya

Another infusion, this one of the vegetable *chaya (see pp68–9)*, best mixed with water and a little lemon juice.

### 9 Licuados

Any kind of fruit – papaya, watermelon, pineapple, mamey, etc – pulped and diluted with water and ice.

### 10 Raspados

Vibrant fruit juices in crushed ice, packed right to the top of the glass.

# AROUND THE YUCATÁN

Left **Xcaret** Center **Waterside restaurant, Cancún** Right **Aviary, Playa del Carmen**

# Cancún and the North

CANCÚN IS THE GREAT MAGNET *at the top of the Mayan Riviera, with lavish hotels, shopping and dining of every kind, wild nightclubs, theme parks, water parks, and other fun things to do spread out along one of the world's finest beaches. To the south is Playa del Carmen, a trendier, more compact style of vacation town, and family-friendly eco-parks that provide an unforgettable introduction to the nature of tropical Yucatán. For a change from resort life, in the same area there are also places where the frenetic pace of modern life still seems delightfully far away – in the ever-mellow Puerto Morelos, at the spectacular bird reserve on Contoy, and on laid-back Isla Mujeres.*

**Señor Frog, Cancún**

## TOP 10 Sights

1. Cancún Beach
2. Cancún Town
3. Isla Mujeres
4. Isla Contoy
5. Holbox
6. Puerto Morelos
7. Punta Bete
8. Tres Ríos
9. Playa del Carmen
10. Xcaret

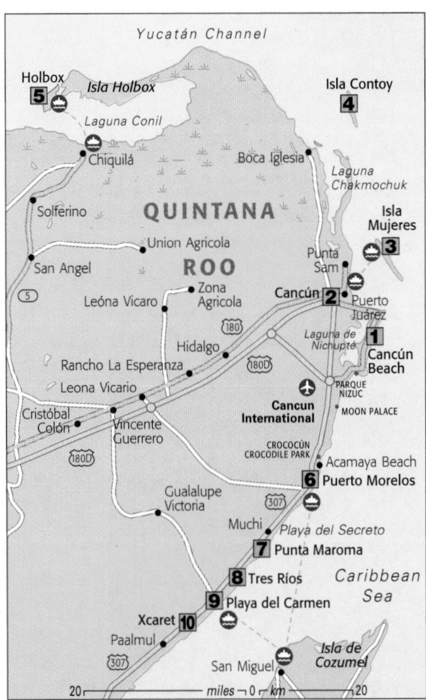

**Lifeguard's hut**



Previous pages **Cancún's Hotel Zone**

Cancún's Hotel Zone

## 1 Cancún Beach

Every one of the Riviera's beaches has the same wonderful fine white sand, which stays deliciously cool to the touch, but Cancún's is unquestionably the finest, stretching the whole 23 km (14 miles) of Cancún Island. Along it, in the Hotel Zone, are resort hotels, shopping and entertainment centers, snorkeling and fun parks, plus the Mayan ruins of El Rey *(see pp8–9)*. *Map L4–K6*

## 2 Cancún Town

On the mainland at the north nd of Cancún Island, Ciudad Cancún, also known as "Downtown," was created at the same time as the Hotel Zone in the 1970s. It's developed an atmosphere of its own, though, and the main drag of Avenida Tulum and the nearby squares and avenues are enjoyable places to explore, with plenty of shopping and great restaurants offering traditional Mexican cooking at low prices *(see pp8–9)*. *Map J3*

## 3 Isla Mujeres

Although it's only a short ferry ride away from Cancún, this 8-km (5-mile) long island, the first place where Spaniards landed in Mexico in 1517, has a very different atmosphere, with few big hotels, one small town, a good choice of cheap places to stay, and a very easy-going, unhurried beach-village feel. Isla is also a great diving, snorkeling, and fishing center, with an exciting range of reefs offshore *(see pp16–17)*. *Map L1–2*

## 4 Isla Contoy

Mexico's most important seabird reserve covers the whole of this uninhabited island. The terrain is a mix of mangroves, beaches, and coral lagoons that are home to over 50 species of birds – they contain turtle breeding grounds too. Day tours are offered by dive shops on Isla Mujeres *(see also pp16–17, 48)*. *Map H1*

Isla Mujeres

## 5 Holbox

This tiny island sits off the north coast of Yucatán, by a wide lagoon full of birds and wild dolphins. On it there's one village with sand streets, a few hotels, pelicans, a huge beach, and an ultra-relaxed, friendly atmosphere. It's wonderful for fishing, clearing the head, and exploring uninhabited islands nearby *(see also p55)*. *Map G1*

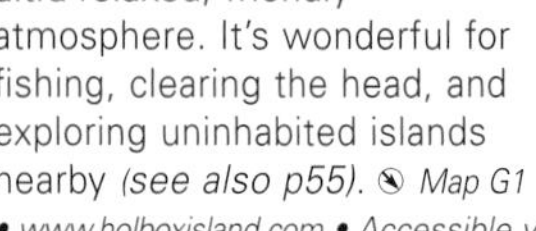

*• www.holboxisland.com • Accessible via Chiquilá, 110 miles (180 km) N of Highway 180; passenger-only ferries cross from Chiquilá to Holbox about every 2 hours (journey time around 20 minutes), 6am–7pm daily*

**Puerto Morelos**

## 6 Puerto Morelos

This little fishing town was the biggest place on this coast before the rise of Cancún. It has avoided overdevelopment and retains a low-key atmosphere, much loved by the many foreigners who own houses here or stay whole winters in its small hotels. There's a beautiful white beach, and a superb reef close offshore (now protected as a marine park) that's wonderful for diving and snorkeling. Local dive operators and fishing guides give individual, friendly service. *Map R3*

### The Chicle Boom

Long before tourism, this region's biggest business was chewing gum. When gum was first invented in the 19th century it was all made with natural chicle, found in the wild sapodilla trees of the Yucatán. Villages like Puerto Juárez and Puerto Morelos were all founded as harbors for exporting chicle, brought in by sapodilla-tappers who roamed the forests inland.

## 7 Punta Bete

Often unnoticed between Puerto Morelos and Playa del Carmen, and kept off the beaten track by a bumpy 3-km (2-mile) access road through the jungle, this point is flanked by long lines of palm-fringed bays – perfect arcs of dazzling white sand by a smooth turquoise sea. They are shared by a few resort hotels, and far more small-scale (and much cheaper) clusters of mellow beach *cabañas* *(see also pp54 & 79)*. *Map R4*

**Punta Bete**

## 8 Tres Ríos

A huge area around a natural inlet and cenote rock pools on the coast has been made into an eco-park, with dense jungle, mangrove lagoons, reefs, and a delicious white beach all within it. Visitors can explore on foot, bicycle, horse-back, or by kayak along

well-marked paths and jungle streams. Other activities include snorkeling, diving, a Kids' Club for small children, and "sensorama", a guided walk using blindfolds, so as to experience the forest by touch and smell alone. *Map R4*
*• www.tres-rios.com • 9am–5pm daily • Adm*

### 9 Playa del Carmen

The Riviera's most vibrant street life, by day and night, and its hippest crowds can be found in its fastest-growing resort town. Playa's long-established cool bars and backpackers' haunts now mix with modern hotels ranging from big resorts to cosy guest houses. As well as having wonderful beaches, it's great for diving and snorkeling *(see pp12–13)*. *Map R4*

### 10 Xcaret

The largest of the Riviera's eco-parks, just south of Playa del Carmen, provides a wonderful introduction to the tropical environment of the Yucatán and a full day's worth of things to do – from snorkeling and swimming with dolphins to eye-popping animal and butterfly collections *(see pp14–15)*. *Map Q4*

Xcaret Mayan Village

## Cancún to Playa

### Morning

Begin by seeing the more traditional side of Cancún with a *desayuno* at one of the **Mercado 28 restaurants** *(see p83)*, in the town market. Then rent a car, head to the Hotel Zone, and drive the length of **Boulevard Kukulcán**.

See something of local history in the **Museo de Antropología** *(see p78)* in the Convention Center, and catch up on Cancún's more glitzy side at the **Forum by the Sea** and **La Isla** complexes *(see p80)*, for some mall-hanging and window-shopping.

Continue down to **El Rey** ruins, to get of an idea of a compact Mayan city; as you leave, walk across the Boulevard to **Playa Delfines**, for crashing surf and a spectacular view north back along Cancún Island and its beach.

### Afternoon

From the end of Boulevard Kukulcán, turn south on Highway 307 and head for **Puerto Morelos**, for a lunch of deliciously refreshing seafood ceviche and a cool beer at **Los Pelícanos** *(see pp70 & 83)*, watching the pelicans hang in the breeze. Rest up on the beach, and take a snorkel so that you can swim over to the Puerto's reef.

Carry on south to **Playa del Carmen**. Check out the beach, and the shops along the Quinta Avenida. If you're staying over in Playa, book a diving or snorkeling trip for the next day. As darkness falls, join the strolling crowds along the Quinta.

Left **El Rey ruins** Center **Crococún Crocodile Park** Right **Playacar aviary**

# TOP 10 Best of the Rest

**1 El Rey Ruins, Cancún**
This was a relatively small Mayan city, but its layout, including a clearly visible "main street", makes it easy to imagine people coming and going, buying and selling. *Map K5 • 8am–5pm daily • Adm*

**2 El Meco Ruins, Cancún**
The ruins of an important Mayan city, probably founded in about AD 300. On its palaces and squat main pyramid are impressive carvings of animals and monsters. *Map K2 • 8am–5pm daily • Adm*

**3 Museo de Antropología e Historia, Cancún**
Ceramics, fine jade and coral jewelry, carvings, and household objects from sites around Quintana Roo state, in engaging, labelled displays. *Map L4 • www.inah.gob.mx • 9am–5pm daily • Adm*

**4 Parque Nizuc, Cancún**
With an interactive dolphin pool, snorkeling with (harmless) stingrays and sharks, as well as a Wet'n'Wild water park, this is the Riviera's biggest fun park *(see also p50). Blvd Kukulcán, km 25 • Map J6 • (998) 193 2000 • www.parquenizuc.com • 10am–5pm daily • Adm*

**5 Puerto Juárez and Punta Sam**
The little passenger (Puerto Juárez) and car (Punta Sam) ferry ports for Isla Mujeres *(see pp16–17)* are older than any other part of Cancún. *Map K1 & 2*

**6 Moon Palace**
One of the largest and best equipped of the Riviera's resort complexes, in its own area of jungle to the south of Cancún. *Map R3 • (998) 881 6000 or (01800) 672 5223 • www.palaceresorts.com*

**7 Acamaya**
A secluded spot to get away from just about everything, set at the end of the bumpy beach road north from Puerto Morelos. There's a small cabaña hotel and a camping site. *Map R3*

**8 Crococún Crocodile Park**
While crocodiles are the key attraction, monkeys and parrots, along with stranger elements of the local wildlife, are also a draw *(see also p58). Highway 307, km 30 • Map R3 • (998) 850 3719 • Summer: 9am–6pm daily (to 5pm in winter) • Adm*

**9 Punta Maroma**
Among the spectacular palm-fringed bays at Punta Maroma are several reserved exclusively for guests at the luxurious tropical retreat of Maroma *(see p127). Map R4*

**10 Playacar**
The plusher side of Playa del Carmen, with a fascinating jungle aviary in the midst of landscaped avenues lined with big resort hotels and private villas *(see also p56). Map Q4*

Left **Playa Tortugas** Right **Playa del Carmen**

# Top 10 Beaches

### 1 Playa Tortugas, Cancún

One of the best beaches on the north side of Cancún Island for mixing with the partying crowds. Highlights include the Fat Tuesday bar (famed for its cocktails), diving, snorkeling, mini-cruises, banana boats, and more. *Blvd Kukulcán, km 5 • Map K4*

### 2 Playa Delfines, Cancún

A great place to find space to stretch out in Cancún, with huge banks of white sand above pounding ocean surf. There's an amazing view north along the beachscape of Cancún Island. *Blvd Kukulcán, km 18 • Map K5*

### 3 Playa Norte, Isla Mujeres

The beach bums' favorite on Isla – a compact strip of white sand with plenty to keep you entertained, from pedalos, kayaks, and snorkeling, to great bars for laid-back socializing under the palms. *Map L1*

### 4 Playa Secreto, Isla Mujeres

Especially good for small kids: a broad, sheltered, shallow inlet tucked away from the main North Beach. Its waters are always tranquil, and the beach is rarely crowded. *Map L1*

### 5 Holbox

One for lovers of real seclusion, with miles of beach from which to pick a spot that's just right. The island faces the opal waters of the Gulf of Mexico, however, so there's no coral *(see also p76)*. *Map G1*

### 6 Puerto Morelos

Excellent for carefree swimming. As well as the fine, uncrowded white sands, there's also a reef full of vivid life just offshore *(see also p76)*. *Map R3*

### 7 Playa del Secreto

A short way south of Puerto Morelos, this big, broad, white sand beach is mostly fronted by private villas, with scarcely any hotels, so there's never any shortage of space. *Map R4*

### 8 Punta Bete

One of the most beautiful spots on the whole Riviera – palms, white sand bays, and turquoise sea. A terrible access road helps keep it that way *(see also p76)*. *Map R4*

### 9 Playa del Carmen

Playa's main town beach is the place to go to survey other sun worshippers, and to show-case your skills at beach volley-ball and other seaside pursuits *(see pp12–13)*. *Map Q4*

### 10 Chunzubul, Playa del Carmen

Keep walking along the beach north from Playa to find endless space, the best snorkeling and diving spots, and nudist beaches. Avoid leaving bags unattended in the really quiet spots *(see also p119)*. *Map Q4*

Left **La Isla, Cancún** Right **Avenida Hidalgo, Isla Mujeres Town**

# Top 10 Places to Shop

### 1 La Isla, Cancún

The latest and most stylish of the Hotel Zone's malls, built as an artificial island surrounded by Venetian-style "canals". It's the place for major fashion names, like DKNY and Dolce e Gabbana. *Blvd Kukulcán, km 12.5 • Map K4*

### 2 Plaza Caracol, Cancún

One of the biggest and most varied of the Cancún malls, with engaging toy shops, lots of beach-wear, fine jewelry stores and a huge choice of restaurants in an attractive, light-filled building. *Blvd Kukulcán, km 8.5 • Map K4*

### 3 La Casa del Arte Mexicano, Cancún

The gift shop at this folk-art museum stocks high-quality crafts from all over Mexico, including some fun toys. *Blvd Kukulcán, km 4 • Map K3*

### 4 Forum by the Sea, Cancún

Shopping highlights here are perfume and jewelry stores and fashion labels like Levi's and Diesel. It also has a huge Hard Rock at its centre, a food court, and clubs alongside. *Blvd Kukulcán, km 9.5 • Map K4 • 10am–midnight daily*

### 5 Coral Negro, Cancún

Not a plush modern mall but a rambling jewelry and handicrafts bazaar, a few steps from the Forum. In among its many stalls you can find fine traditional craftwork, as well as a lot of junk. *Boulevard Kukulcán, km 9.5 • Map L4*

### 6 Mercado 23, Cancún

This little open-air market is a colorful destination where locals go to shop for meat, vegetables, herbal cures, and even party supplies and piñatas. *Off Avenida Tulum on Calle Cedro • Map J3*

### 7 Mercado 28, Cancún

The town market is the place for old-style shopping – giant stands of *huarache* sandals and panama hats, and tables full of fresh vegetables and fruit – plus a great food court *(see p83)*. *Av Xel-Ha and Av Tankah • Map J3*

### 8 Avenida Hidalgo, Isla Mujeres Town

Isla's main street, and its main drag for leisurely browsing. Here and in parallel Av Juárez small shops offer painted wooden birds, original T-shirts and local shell and coral jewelry. *Map L1*

### 9 Super Telas, Playa del Carmen

Fine quality Mexican textiles (*telas*), in traditional or original designs, can be found here. A more original shop than most around Playa's Quinta Avenida. *Constituyentes, Plaza Las Perlas • Map Q4*

### 10 Caracol, Playa del Carmen

The specialities at this two-storey boutique are textiles and embroidery from all over Mexico – particularly Chiapas – and from Guatemala. *Av 5, between Calle 6 and Calle 84 • Map Q4*

Left **Coco Bongo** Center **Azúcar** Right **La Santanera**

# TOP 10 Nightclubs

**1 Coco Bongo, Cancún**
Cancún's most high-tech, high-powered, multilevel mega-club, with a wide-ranging music menu *(see p60)*. *Blvd Kukulcán, km 9.5 • Map L4 • (998) 883 0592 • From 10:30pm daily • Adm*

**2 Bulldog, Cancún**
On weekends, sharply dressed local kids gather in front of the Bulldog's entry staircase, waiting to get in and dance to hip-hop and *rock en español (see p60)*. *Blvd Kukulcán, km 8 • Map L4 • (998) 848 9800 • 11pm–4am daily • Adm*

**3 Dady'O, Cancún**
The college crowd's favorite holds bikini nights and other rowdy fun. Dady Rock, next door, often hosts live bands *(see p60)*. *Blvd Kukulcán, km 9.5 • Map L4 • (998) 883 3333 • Dady'O from 10pm daily, Dady Rock from 6pm daily • Adm*

**4 The City**
This huge, modern nightclub also contains a beach club, bar, restaurant, and lounge. *Blvd Kukulcán, km 9.5 • Map L4 • (998) 848 8380 • Nightclub open from 10pm daily • Casual dress but no sandals or bathing suits • Adm*

**5 Captain Hook's Pirate Night, Cancún**
Dinner cruises are normally more sedate than clubbing in Cancún, but Captain Hook's is still pretty boisterous, with a "pirate" crew staging a battle *(see p60)*. *El Embarcadero, Blvd Kukulcán, km 4.5 • Map K3 • From 7pm daily • From 7pm daily • Adm*

**6 Azúcar, Cancún**
The best place in Cancún to dance to live salsa, Afro-Latin merengue and other rhythms *(see pp62–3)*. *Punta Cancún, next to Hotel Dreams Cancún • Map L4 • (998) 848 7000 (ext 7980) • From 9pm Mon–Sat*

**7 Pat O'Brien's, Cancún**
Famous for its cocktails, this nightclub boasts an outdoor patio, sports bar, and live music. *Flamingo Plaza, Blvd Kukulcán, km 11.5 • Map L4 • Open 7am–2am daily • Adm*

**8 La Santanera, Playa del Carmen**
A two-story club offering two venues in one. Each night DJs play electronica and house music *(see p61)*. *Calle 4, between Av 5 and Av 12 • Map Q4 • (984) 803 2856 • From 11pm daily • Adm*

**9 Blue Parrot Beach Club, Playa del Carmen**
Dance under the stars at this beachfront club split into two separate venues. DJs perform nightly. *Calle 12 Norte • Map Q4 • (984) 873 0083 • From 11pm daily • Adm*

**10 Mambo Café, Playa del Carmen**
If you like to dance to classic tropical sounds mixed with brand-new Latin pop, this is the place for you. *Calle 6 Norte • Map Q4 • From 10pm Tue–Sun • Adm*

Left **La Madonna** Center **Señor Frog's** Right **Mamita's Beach Club**

# TOP 10 Drinking and Entertainment Spots

### 1 La Madonna, Cancún

A strikingly elegant bar-restaurant in Cancún's smartest mall, La Isla, with decor that's a hybrid of Baroque and Art Nouveau. *La Isla, Blvd Kukulcán, km 12.5 • Map K4 • $$$*

### 2 Señor Frog's, Cancún

Beside Laguna Nichupté, this is one of the most popular Cancún outlets of the Anderson group *(see p61)*. Party atmosphere, often with rock bands, guaranteed. *Blvd Kukulcán, km 9.5 • Map L4 • $$*

### 3 Hard Rock, Cancún

Looking a bit like a giant Roman temple, Cancún's Hard Rock is impossible to miss. The rock'n'roll bar formula is familiar worldwide, but this one is a real crowd-puller. *Forum by the Sea, Blvd Kukulcán, km 9.5 • Map L4 • $$$*

### 4 Roots, Cancún

A dark, Boho-ish little bar with a Latin-jazz soundtrack. Roots offers the promise of "food, music, and art". There's a clutch of other intimate, buzzing bars on the same street, just off Avenida Tulum. *Calle Tulipanes 25 • Map J3 • $*

### 5 Buho's, Isla Mujeres

Isla's funkiest beach bar. With a palm roof to give shade, it's right on the sand, just steps away from the sea, and offers Mexican snacks to go with the cocktails and chilled beers. *Playa Norte • Map L1 • $$*

### 6 El Café Cito, Isla Mujeres

This mellow place, a few streets from the beach, offers excellent breakfasts and superior coffee and fresh juice combos later in the day. *Av Juárez, corner of Av Matamoros, Isla Town • Map L1 • $*

### 7 Mamita's Beach Club, Playa del Carmen

One of the nicest beaches in Playa is also the most popular daytime party spot, with lounge beds and hammocks for rent alongside the usual chairs, a DJ, and strong Margaritas. *On the beach at Calle 28 • Map Q4 • $$*

### 8 Fly, Playa del Carmen

A spectacular chrome-and-glass bar that wouldn't be out of place in New York or Miami Beach. Luminous house cocktails are the cool specialty. *Deseo Hotel, Av 5, by Calle 12 • Map Q4 • $$*

### 9 Pez Vela, Playa del Carmen

Ever popular bar-restaurant with a huge outside terrace that's one of the fixtures on the Quinta Avenida promenade. The style is hippy-Caribbean, helped along by chugging reggae and rock bands. *Av 5, by Calle 2 • Map Q4 • $*

### 10 Diablito Cha Cha Cha, Playa del Carmen

With comfortable sofas and a stylish clientele, this is the place to warm up before hitting the bigger dance clubs *(see p61)*. *Calle 12 at Av 1 Norte • Map Q4 • $$*

**Price Categories**

| For a three-course meal for one with a beer or soda (or equivalent meal), taxes and extra charges. | |
|---|---|
| $ | under $5 |
| $$ | $5–$10 |
| $$$ | $10–$20 |
| $$$$ | $20–$35 |
| $$$$$ | over $35 |

Left **La Habichuela** Right **La Parrilla**

# TOP 10 Places to Eat

### 1 JC Capitán, Cancún

This seafood restaurant overlooking the lagoon is beautiful at sunset, and a great place to try spicy *camaronillas* (fried shrimp in tortillas). *Blvd Kukulcán, km 19.6 • Map K6 • (998) 885 3126 • $$$$*

### 2 La Habichuela, Cancún

A charming specialist in Yucatecan and Mexican tropical seafood in a softly lit garden by the tranquil Parque de las Palapas *(see p70)*. *Calle Margaritas 25 • Map J3 • (998) 884 3158 • $$$$$*

### 3 La Parrilla, Cancún

La Parrilla offers a good range of Mexican favorites such as grilled meats, soups, and fondues. Daily mariachi music creates a warm atmosphere *(see p70)*. *Av Yaxchilán 51 • Map J3 • (998) 884 5398 • $$$$*

### 4 La Cueva del Pirata, Isla Holbox

Handmade pasta, shrimp, loads of garlic, and a convivial Italian chef-owner combine to make this one of the nicest restaurants on this island. *West side of the plaza • Map G1 • (984) 875 2183 • $$$$*

### 5 Mercado 28 Restaurants, Cancún

The courtyard of the town market is packed with canopied tables spilling out from restaurants. The traditional food served, such as *pollo con mole* *(see p69)* is fun and cheap. *Av Xel-Ha and Av Tankah • Map J3 • No credit cards • $$*

### 6 Manolo's, Isla Mujeres

In a pretty garden patio, this charming, family-run restaurant is delightfully relaxing. On the menu are classic Yucatecan seafood dishes. *Av Juárez, between Matamoros and Abasolo, Isla Town • Map L1 • No credit cards • $$$*

### 7 Los Pelícanos, Puerto Morelos

One of the all-time best beach-terrace restaurants, a wonderful place to linger over its renowned seafood cocktails, or one of the subtle fish dishes *(see p70)*. *On the Plaza • Map R3 • $$$*

### 8 La Casa del Agua, Playa del Carmen

This stylish café-restaurant-gallery surveys the Quinta Avenida bustle from an airy balcony. The menu features an imaginative, Mexican-European mix. *Av 5, by Calle 2 • Map Q4 • (984) 803 0232 • $$$$*

### 9 John Gray's Place, Playa del Carmen

Whether upstairs in the dining room or downstairs at the bar, John Gray's delivers excellent food in a warmly lit, minimalist setting *(see p71)*. *Calle Corazon, off Av 5 • Map Q4 • (984) 803 3689 • $$$$$*

### 10 Coctelería Las Brisas, Playa del Carmen

This big terrace-restaurant has a straightforward style, but its fresh local seafood is some of the best in town. *Calle 4, between Av 5 and Av 10 • Map Q4 • No credit cards • $$*

***Note:** Unless otherwise stated, all restaurants serve vegetarian meals; phone numbers included only where appropriate*

Left **Snorkeling** Center **Puerto Aventuras** Right **Tulum**

# Cozumel and the South

THE SOUTHERN STRETCH OF THE RIVIERA *is the less publicized, less built-up part of this coast, but still offers the choice between luxury resorts and out-of-the-way places – except that here the resorts are not so hectic, and the untouched corners are more remote. Offshore, Cozumel is a super-relaxing island that offers fantastic diving opportunities. Onshore are some of the Caribbean's most dazzling tropical beaches, such as the seven bays of Xpu-Ha and the crescent of Media Luna Bay. They lead down the coast to the great beach refuge of Tulum, with its Mayan temple ruins. A little way inland is another great Mayan site, the forest-clad city of Cobá.*

## Top 10 Sights

1. **Cozumel**
2. **The Cozumel Reefs**
3. **San Gervasio, Cozumel**
4. **Puerto Aventuras**
5. **Xpu-Ha**
6. **Akumal**
7. **Xel-Ha**
8. **Tulum**
9. **Cobá**
10. **Sian Ka'an**

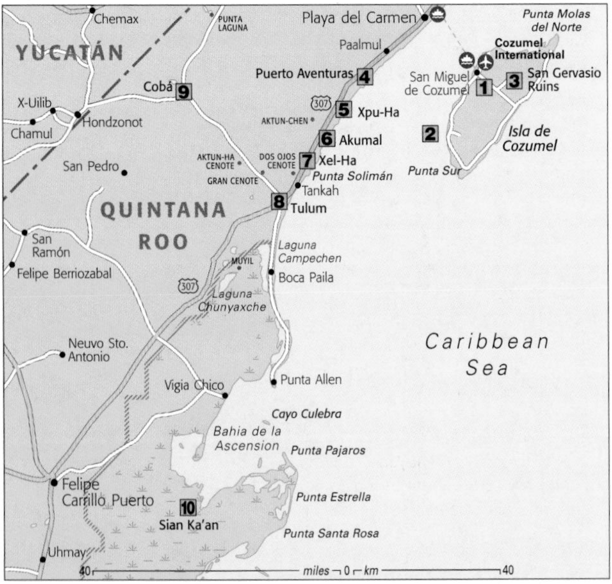

Previous pages **Monastery of San Antonio, Izamal** ***(see p99)***

Laguna Chankanaab, one of Cozumel's shoreline reefs

## 1 Cozumel

Gleaming jewelry stores along the waterfront in San Miguel combine with an easy-going, small-town charm that has long made this island a favorite with families. It's a great place to settle into at a leisurely pace, maybe going diving one day, then exploring a little the next: around the island are Mayan ruins, windblown cliffs, a fascinating natural wildlife park at Punta Sur, and lovely beaches and snorkeling spots on the west coast *(see pp10–11)*. *Map R5*

## 2 The Cozumel Reefs

Cozumel's greatest glory is its 20-plus coral reefs, an awe-inspiring undersea world of caves, canyons, and coral "forests" teeming with life – from sea cucumbers and brilliantly luminous angelfish to graceful rays and the occasional shark. The water boasts almost perfect clarity, and Chankanaab and Paraíso reefs are close inshore, so can be appreciated even by inexperienced divers and snorkelers *(see p11)*.

## 3 San Gervasio, Cozumel

The ruins of the Mayan capital of Cozumel, conquered by Cortés and his Spanish soldiers in 1519, are in the middle of the island. Its buildings are small compared to the great Mayan cities, but there are many of them – and discovering them, through woods full of wonderful scents, flowers, and birds, involves a lovely walk *(see p11)*. *Map R5 • (998) 849 2885 • 8am–5pm daily • Adm*

## 4 Puerto Aventuras

The biggest, most opulent resort on the southern Riviera, a specially created vacation village around an inlet that's now a pretty pleasure port lined with shops and restaurants. The nine-hole golf course is attractive, and the marina is the best-equipped on the whole Riviera, making it a popular base for serious deep-sea fishing enthusiasts. In another part of the harbor you can swim with dolphins *(see p50)*. *Map Q5*

San Gervasio ruins

## 5 Xpu-Ha

Tulum coast

Along these seven gracefully sweeping bays, 3 km (2 miles) south of Puerto Aventuras, are some of the Riviera's most idyllic beaches, with exuberantly alive reefs and some of the most exquisite turquoise waters. Several are now occupied by resort complexes (the Xpu-Ha Palace, the Copacabana, Robinson Club). However, two (signposted X-4 and X-7 from the Highway), are still open to anyone, and at X-7 there are some small *cabañas*, a camping site, and a dive shop. *Map P5*

## 6 Akumal

Long a favorite dive destination, with fabulous reefs and places for cave diving, Akumal has grown a good deal without being overwhelmed. It spreads over several long, lovely bays – Media Luna is the most beautiful, with the delightful Yal-Ku lagoon *(see p59)*. There are more apartments, villas, and small hotels than big developments, so it's still quite easy to find secluded spots – certainly the turtles try to, and the beaches near Akumal village are favorite breeding grounds. *Map P5*

### The Sacbé of Cobá

Cobá was the center of the largest network of *sacbé*, or Mayan stone roads, in the Mayan world. They connected the parts of the city, as well as vassal-cities. About AD 800 Cobá built the longest ever *sacbé*, of over 100 km (60 miles), to Yaxuná in the west, to help reinforce it in the wars with Chichén – unsuccessfully, as Cobá was defeated shortly afterward.

## 7 Xel-Ha

One of the most luxuriant coral inlets on the coast has been made a "snorkel park" that's one of the Riviera's most popular attractions – experienced divers may find it tame, but the easy snorkeling is great for families. Around it is a forest park and a beach. Just outside the park and across the Highway are the Mayan ruins of Xel-Ha *(see p90)*.
*Map P6 • (998) 883 0524 • www.xelha.com. • 8am–6pm daily (to 7pm in summer) • Adm*

Xel-Ha

## 8 Tulum

A ruined temple of a Mayan city, the Castillo, rises up on a crag above a long, long palm-fringed beach, interrupted by rocks and curving


*For the best beaches on Cozumel and around the south* **see p91**

headlands as it stretches 11 km (7 miles) down to Sian Ka'an. All along it are clusters of palm-roofed cabins. There's good diving and fishing offshore, and around it is one of the best areas in the world for cave diving *(see pp52–3)*. *Map P6*

### 9 Cobá

This huge Mayan city – once home to around 50,000 people – was the great rival of Chichén Itzá. It's a very different place to visit from Chichén Itzá or Uxmal – it's unusually spread out around several large lakes, and to find its massive buildings you follow fascinating walks through thick forest full of birds and plants. Yucatán's tallest pyramid is here *(see also p38)*. *Map M5*

*• www.inah.gob.mx • 8am–5pm • Adm*

### 10 Sian Ka'an

Mexico's largest wetland nature reserve, Sian Ka'an brings the Riviera to an end just south of Tulum. Its vast area of nearly untouched mangroves, jungle, and beaches contains an extraordinary range of birds and wildlife, and the one-day tours run by local organizations give a glimpse of the intricate, constantly surprising interplay of nature in this rare environment. The few inhabited spots along the coast are wonderful for fishing, and have a feel of tranquil isolation *(see also pp20–21)*. *Map F6*

**Sian Ka'an reserve**

## Cozumel in a day

### Morning

Start with breakfast, coffee, or a drink at **Las Palmeras** *(see p94)*, watching the new arrivals off the Playa del Carmen ferry. Browse in the jewelry and souvenir shops along the waterfront and in the streets around the square, but don't buy anything yet. Rent a car and head out of town down Avenida Juárez to the Mayan ruins of **San Gervasio**. If you hire the services of a guide at the entrance don't let them hurry you, but take time to notice the birds and vegetation – as much of an attraction as the ruins.

Back at the main road, head left to meet the east coast at windswept **Punta Santa Cecilia**. Turn south down the road beside the rocks and waves for a lunch of mixed fish and seafood on the beach at **Chen Río** *(see p95)*.

### Afternoon

Carry on down the coast to **Parque Punta Sur**. From the parking lot, walk down to Punta Celarain lighthouse and the strange little Mayan temple called the Caracol, and follow the nature trail to try and see some crocodiles and flamingos.

You can snorkel at Punta Sur, but you're likely to see more underwater life if you carry on to **Laguna Chankanaab** *(p87)*. If all you want is a placid beach, call in at **Playa San Francisco** *(p91)*. Roll back into town, and don't miss the sunset from the waterfront Malecón. Take another look at the shops, and buy anything you may have spotted on your morning walk.

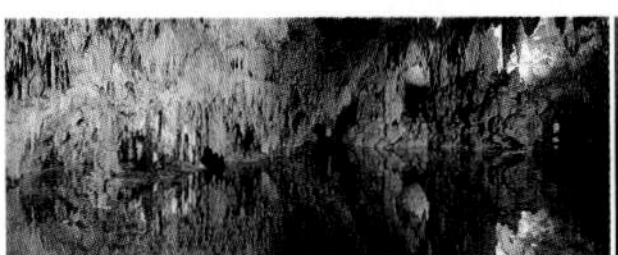

Left **Aktun-Chen** Right **Punta Laguna**

# TOP 10 Best of the Rest

**1 Paamul**
The favorite destination for RV travelers, who take advantage of generous long-term rates to settle in for the whole winter. The campsite also has *cabañas* *(see p126)*, a beach bar *(p91)*, and a dive shop. *Map Q5*

**2 Aktun-Chen Cave**
This giant cave and cenote system, an awesome series of chambers and stalagmite towers, is in thick jungle in a nature park; it was only recently discovered. *(see p51)*. *Map P5*

**3 Xel-Ha Ruins**
Across the Highway from the popular snorkel park, this ruined Mayan city is one of the oldest in the region. On some buildings there are murals dating back to about AD 200. *Map P6 • 8am–6pm daily (summer 9am–7pm) • Adm*

**4 Tankah**
Off the beaten track, Tankah is a placid, narrow beach with a fine reef, a restaurant, and a small cluster of villas and hotels. Just behind the beach by the Casa Cenote restaurant, there's a broad, reed-lined cenote, so it's a toss-up between swimming in the surf or the freshwater pool. *Map P6*

**5 Dos Ojos Cenote and Hidden Worlds**
Dos Ojos is very possibly the world's longest underwater cave system. The snorkeling or diving tours offered by the Hidden Worlds center are a memorable experience *(see p51)*. *Map P6*

**6 Gran Cenote**
The Cobá road north from Tulum is one of the best places to find swimmable cenotes, and this is one of the most beautiful, a crystal-clear pool that's a must for swimmers and snorkelers *(see p52)*. *Map N6*

**7 Aktun-Ha Cenote**
Another fine swimming-hole cenote amid rocks and woods toward Cobá. Snorkelers can explore the huge main cavern; divers (with guides) can go further. *Map N6*

**8 Punta Laguna**
In a tiny village by a forest lake north of Cobá, this nature reserve is one of the best places to see spider monkeys in the Yucatán. Villagers act as guides *(see p48)*. *Map N4*

**9 Muyil Ruins**
Location is the attraction of this old, atmospheric Mayan city: in hot, steamy jungle between the Highway and Lake Chunyaxché, in the Sian Ka'an reserve. *Map G4 • 8am–5pm daily • Adm*

**10 Road from Boca Paila to Punta Allen**
One for the adventurous – one of the bumpiest, most rutted, overgrown and deserted roads in the Yucatán – with fabulous vistas of sea, sky, and forest. *Map G4–5*

Left **Playa Sol** Center **North Beach, Tulum** Right **South Beach, Tulum**

# TOP 10 Beaches

### 1 Playa San Francisco and Playa Sol, Cozumel

Two among the many great beaches on Cozumel's southwest coast: San Francisco and others near it are great for all-round relaxation; Playa Sol is best if you want a beach with loads going on. *Map R6*

### 2 Chen Río, Cozumel

The best beach on Cozumel's rugged eastern shore, with a sheltered cove for lazy swimming, while further along the sands you could even surf. There's also a beach restaurant worth a special visit *(see p70)*. *Map R5*

### 3 Paamul

A curving white sand bay with a likable beach bar and *cabañas (see p126)*. With over 2 km (1 mile) of beach, the camp site doesn't obstruct the view, and the sands are never crowded. *Map Q5*

### 4 Xpu-Ha

Seven bays with some of the coolest, whitest sand, most graceful palms, and most colorful coral on the Riviera. Several are occupied by resorts, but X-4 and X-7, signposted on the Highway, are open to anyone. *Map P5*

### 5 Media Luna Bay, Akumal

As the name suggests, "Half Moon Bay" is an exquisite, near-perfect crescent of brilliant white sand and calm sea. The atmosphere is just as tranquil: around it there are condos and villas, and at the north end is the lovely Yal-Ku lagoon *(see p59)*. d *Map P5*

### 6 Akumal Village

The beach in the center of Akumal is a little busier, and behind it there's a bigger choice of low-key bars and shops. *Map P5*

### 7 Punta Solimán

Shaded by lolling palms, this near-empty beach feels far from anywhere, even though it's only a dirt-track away from the Highway. A few boats on the sand and the bar *(see p94)* are the main signs of habitation. *Map P6*

### 8 North Beach, Tulum

The beaches at the north end of Tulum are the favorites for anyone who wants to hang out and get to know people in the bargain-basement *cabañas*. They also have the best view of the ruins *(see p18)*. *Map P6*

### 9 South Beach, Tulum

The place for people who want to find some seclusion in Tulum, with longer, broader, whiter beaches, acres of space, and quite luxurious comforts in some *cabañas*. *Map P6*

### 10 Punta Xamach & Conoco

Getting to these remote, deserted beaches involves negotiating the wild, rutted road between Boca Paila and Punta Allen *(see p90)*. So, whether this appeals or not may depend on your vehicle. *Map G5*

Left **Punta Langosta** Center **Los Cinco Soles** Right **Puerto Aventuras**

# Top 10 Places to Shop

**1 Punta Langosta, Cozumel**
The most gleaming addition to Cozumel shopping, the leisure mall in the cruise terminal has major international fashion names – Versace, Tommy Hilfiger – plus upscale handicrafts and glittering gem stores. *Map R5*

**2 Inspiración Gallery, Cozumel**
This small gallery displays a fine selection of handicrafts as well as local photography, paintings and jewelry. A great place to pick up one-of-a-kind gifts. *Av Rafael Melgar, between Av Juárez and Calle 2 Norte • Map R5*

**3 Rachat & Romero, Cozumel**
A more cluttered Malecón jewelry store that's also a bit less traditional in its styles and designs. Among its displays are beautiful pieces in Mexican jade, jet, and amber. *Av 5 Sur, between Av Salas and Calle 1 • Map R5*

**4 Miró T-Shirts, Cozumel**
Miró company's T-shirts stand out with their distinctive, stylish, bright and very Mexican designs, which justify the slightly higher prices. Their Cozumel store is next to Las Palmeras *(see p94)*. *Av Rafael Melgar–Plaza Cozumel • Map R5*

**5 Los Cinco Soles, Cozumel**
The place to do all your souvenir shopping in one go – a giant Malecón handicrafts store. Tablecloths, clothes, jewelry, glassware, metal or papier-mâché birds and animals, and more. *Av Rafael Melgar 27, by Calle 8 • Map R5*

**6 Unicornio, Cozumel**
A big, varied crafts dealer, with especially good ceramics and painted wood. There's junk as well as quality pieces, but it's a great place to browse. *Av 5 Sur, near Calle 1 Sur • Map R5*

**7 Shalom, Tulum**
Get dressed for a Tulum-style beach party at this cool shop that features hippie-style clothing as well as sleeker items that you could wear when out clubbing. *Av Tulum, between Calle Orion and Calle Centauro • Map N6*

**8 Pro Dive, Cozumel**
First port of call for self-sufficient divers and sea-explorers on Cozumel, with every possible kind of diving and snorkeling equipment. *Av Adolfo Rosado Salas 198, corner of Av 5 • Map R5*

**9 Puerto Aventuras**
A small, stylish group of shops. Among cigars and sophisticated jewelry, you'll also find Mexican designer clothing at Arte Maya and fine handicrafts at El Guerrero. *Map Q5*

**10 Mixik Artesanías, Tulum**
Tulum is not a shopping mecca, but this little store has a high-quality collection of colorful craftwork from every part of Mexico. *Av Tulum, opposite the bus terminal • Map P6*

Left **Carlos'n'Charlie's** Right **Jane's Sports and Sorts**

# Top 10 Nightspots

**1 Carlos 'n' Charlie's, Cozumel**
Cozumel's biggest bar-restaurant-music venue is the place where you're assured of finding a (usually pretty raucous) crowd every night, partying in the open air to classic rock circa 1970 to 2000 *(see p61)*. *Punta Langosta • Map R5 • daily from 3pm*

**2 Neptuno, Cozumel**
Top of the line in Cozumel dance clubs – the only one that's really hi-tech. The music menu is a mix of Latin and international dance and there's a dazzling laser and light show. *Av Rafael Melgar, by Calle 11 • Map R5 • daily from 10pm*

**3 Plaza del Sol, Cozumel**
Cozumel doesn't have a particularly wild nightlife. Instead, San Miguel's central plaza is the place to be – especially on Sundays, when there's usually live music. *Av Melgar at Av Juárez • Map R5*

**4 La Zebra, Tulum**
La Zebra's Sunday night salsa party draws people from up and down the beach as well as from town. Come early for free dance classes. *Beach road, km 4.6 • Map G4*

**5 Hard Rock Café, Cozumel**
The Mayan-style architecture of the building makes this a s tunning location for the rock memorabilia chain. Occasional live music. *Av Rafeal E Melgar 2A • Map R5 • daily from 10pm • Adm*

**6 El Manatí, Cozumel**
In the back garden of a wooden Caribbean-style house, this restaurant turns into a dance club on weekends, when local rock, salsa and reggae bands get the enthusiastic crowd dancing. *Av 10 Norte at Calle 8 • Map R5 • 9.30pm–12.30am daily*

**7 Jane's Sports and Sorts, Puerto Aventuras**
Big and comfortable bar with a convivial, boisterous feel where you can keep up with U.S. sports and party on into the night. *On the Marina • Map Q5 • daily from 3pm*

**8 Capricho, Puerto Aventuras**
Puerto Aventuras' own disco-bar is unpredictable – sometimes quiet, sometimes buzzing. The music is eclectic. *On the Marina • Map Q5 • Thu–Sun from 10pm • Adm*

**9 Acabar, Tulum**
A casual split-level space, Acabar is the main late-night hangout in the town of Tulum. It features live reggae bands, cheap drinks and billiards and foosball tables. *Av Tulum between Calle Orion and Calle Beta • Map P6*

**10 Mezzanine, Tulum**
This stylish restaurant-bar combines luxurious indulgence with eco-friendly policies. Enjoy a cocktail while chilling to the sounds of guest DJs. *Carretera Boca Paila km 1.5 • Map P6 • daily from 11am • No credit cards • Adm*

Left **Las Palmeras** Center **Piña Colada** Right **El Paraíso**

# TOP 10 Drinking and Entertainment Spots

**1 Hard Rock, Cozumel**
Cozumel's Hard Rock offers no changes from the international formula but draws in the crowds with its loud, friendly atmosphere. Special pluses are good air-con and better live bands than most island bars. *Av Rafael Melgar 2A, by Av Juárez • Map R5 • $$*

**2 Las Palmeras, Cozumel**
A big, friendly, Caribbean-hut of a bar, opposite the ferry landing on San Miguel's main plaza. As well as being great for drinks and people-watching, it does highly enjoyable breakfasts. *Av Rafael Melgar–Plaza Cozumel • Map R5 • $$*

**3 Kelley's, Cozumel**
Popular with divemasters and tour guides, this outdoor bar can get rowdy when an American football game is on. It's the ideal spot for a cold beer and a hamburger. *Av 10, between Av Salas and Calle 1 • Map R5 • $*

**4 Havana Blue, Cozumel**
One of the few bars with a sea view in San Miguel, Havana Blue also looks great on the inside, with sleek blue booths for lounging with drinks while the sun goes down. *Forum Shops, Av Melgar at Calle 10 • Map R5 • $$*

**5 Café del Museo, Cozumel**
This very relaxing, pretty café on the roof of Cozumel's museum *(see p10)* has a great view of the waterfront and good coffee. Tasty breakfasts and snacks too. *Av Rafael Melgar, by Calle 4 • Map R5 • 9am–5pm daily • $*

**6 Mezcalito's, Cozumel**
An old favorite, ultra-laid-back beach restaurant in a wonderful location where the cross-island road meets the east coast, with a soundtrack of crashing surf. *Punta Santa Cecilia • Map R5 • $*

**7 Cabañas Paamul**
Deep shade and an ideal view over the beach make the bar in the Paamul cabañas and camping site *(see p126)* a great place to get refreshed after time in the sun. Snacks are also available. *Map Q5 • $*

**8 Piña Colada, Puerto Aventuras**
Puerto Aventuras' favorite beach bar, with a big palapa roof. Elaborate tropical cocktails are the specialty. *Map Q5 • $$*

**9 Oscar y Lalo, Punta Solimán**
Punta Solimán has a desert-island feel, and so does its only bar. Hosts Oscar and Lalo, who also run the camping site and rent kayaks, are friendly and cook great fresh seafood. *Map P6 • $*

**10 El Paraíso, Tulum**
Many of the cabaña-clusters along Tulum beach have bars, but Paraíso, near the ruins, has the best view, with a big terrace for catching the breeze. *Beach road km 5.5 • Map P6 • $$*

**Price Categories**

| For a three-course meal for one with a beer or soda (or equivalent meal), taxes, and extra charges. | | |
|---|---|---|
| | **$** | under $5 |
| | **$$** | $5–$10 |
| | **$$$** | $10–$20 |
| | **$$$$** | $20–$35 |
| | **$$$$$** | over $35 |

Left **Guido's** Right **Rock'n Java**

# TOP 10 Places to Eat

### 1 Guido's, Cozumel

Guido's is best known for its rich lasagne, but its other Italian food, including wood-oven pizzas, is great too. Enjoy it all outside in the garden. *Av Melgar No.23, between Calle 6 and Calle 8 • Map R5 • (987) 872 0946 • $$$$*

### 2 Rock'n Java, Cozumel

The big fresh salads and sandwiches are great at this American-run café on the water. Save some room for a huge slice of apple pie or one of the other gooey desserts. *Av Rafael Melgar No.602, between Calle 7 and Av Quintana Roo • Map R5 • (987) 872 4405 • $$$*

### 3 Casa Denis, Cozumel

One of the island's oldest restaurants in a wooden house just off the square, Casa Denis serves classic Yucatecan dishes *(see pp68–9)* at low prices. *Calle 1 Sur, by Av 5 • Map R5 • from 7am daily • No credit cards • $$$*

### 4 La Cocay, Cozumel

This mellow restaurant in a Caribbean-style wooden hut offers a range of Mediterranean-inspired dishes, including pasta, light fish specialties, and excellent salads. *Calle 8, between Av 10 and Av 15 • Map R5 • $$$$*

### 5 Chen Río, Cozumel

The best restaurant on Cozumel's east coast, and a wonderful place to eat on the beach *(see p70)*. *Chen Río Beach • Map R5 • No credit cards • $$$*

### 6 Richard's Steaks and Pizza, Puerto Aventuras

This restaurant is located in a cabaña with a sea view. The menu offers a variety of typical American and Mexican dishes. *Centro Comercial Marina • Map Q5 • (984) 873 5086 • $$$$*

### 7 Qué Onda, Akumal

Run by a charming Mexican–Italian couple, this relaxing garden restaurant has a varied and international menu, with great light lunches. *Near north end of Media Luna Bay road • Map P5 • (984) 875 9101 • $$$*

### 8 Cetli, Tulum

A Mexico City-trained chef-owner turns out light, refined versions of Mexican classics like *chiles en nogada* (stuffed chilies with walnut sauce) at this casual eatery. *Calle Polar at Calle Orion • Map P6 • (984) 108 0681 • $$$*

### 9 Don Cafeto, Tulum

One of Tulum's longest-established restaurants, with a big outdoor terrace, and one of the best places for traditional Mexican dishes. *Av Tulum, three blocks north of baseball field • Map P6 • (984) 871 2207 • $$$*

### 10 Urge Taquitos, Tulum

Beer-batter shrimp and fish tacos are flawlessly cooked at this roadside stop. Pile them high with toppings from the salsa and condiment bars. *Hwy-307 north of town • Map P6 • $$*

***Note:** Unless otherwise stated, all restaurants serve vegetarian meals; phone numbers included only where appropriate*

Left **Ek-Balam** Right **Flamingos, Río Lagartos**

# Central Heartland

AN UNMISTAKABLE YUCATECAN IDENTITY *and sense of their own culture distinguishes towns like Valladolid or Tizimín, with Spanish colonial churches and squares, Mayan women selling colorful fruit and flowers, and a gently paced street life. The ancestors of the modern Maya built some of their greatest creations here, at Ek-Balam and the city of Chichén Itzá. Giant underground caverns and magical cenote pools lie beneath the landscape.*

**Cenote Dzitnup**

## TOP 10 Sights in Central Yucatan

1. Valladolid
2. San Bernardino Sisal, Valladolid
3. Cenote Dzitnup
4. Ek-Balam
5. Balankanché Caves
6. Chichén Itzá
7. Río Lagartos
8. San Felipe
9. Izamal
10. Telchac and Uaymitún

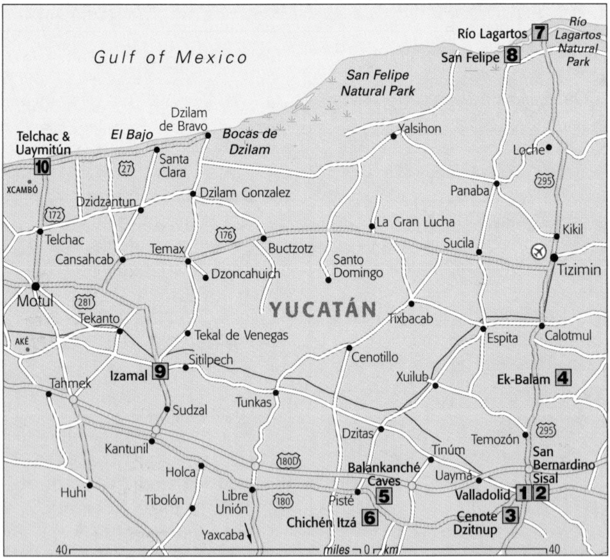

Valladolid

## 1 Valladolid

The Spanish capital of eastern Yucatán, founded in 1545, has at its heart one of the most charming of the region's colonial plazas – wonderful for people-watching – overlooked by the tall white cathedral. Valladolid is celebrated for embroidery, and the square is a good place to buy the white, flower-patterned *huípil* dresses and tablecloths. Around the town there are many more fine old Spanish churches and houses, and just four blocks from the plaza you can look down into the dramatic pit of Cenote Zací, once Valladolid's water source. ✎ *Map E3*

## 2 San Bernardino Sisal, Valladolid

This massive, fortress-like church and cloister was begun in 1552, and is the oldest permanent church in the Yucatán. Like others built around that time, it was designed by the Franciscan order's own architect, Friar Juan de Mérida. It looks very medieval, with an unusual, beautifully shady gallery of graceful arches along the façade and a cloister of giant, squat stone columns around an exuberantly overgrown garden. Church and cloister have a delightful tranquility, and inside there are rare 18th-century Baroque altars and altarpieces *(see also p42)*. ✎ *Map E3 • Calle 41–A, Valladolid • 8am–noon, 5–7pm Mon, Wed–Sun • Adm occasionally*

## 3 Cenote Dzitnup

This is the most spectacular of the easily accessible, swimmable cenotes, and one of the great sights of the Yucatán. Entering through a cramped tunnel, you emerge into a vast, cathedral-like cavern, with towers of strangely shaped rock around an exquisite turquoise pool. In the middle, a shaft of sunlight falls dead straight onto the water from a hole in the roof. Everyone automatically swims through it, to be touched by this magical light *(see also p52)*. ✎ *Dzitnup village • Map E3 • 8am–5pm daily • Adm*

San Bernardino Sisal, Valladolid

Ek-Balam

### The Salt of Chichén

Salt was one of the greatest sources of wealth in ancient America. In the lagoons near Río Lagartos there are huge salt flats, still exploited today. Around AD 800, Chichén Itzá won control of them and built its own port at El Cerritos, east of Río Lagartos, to trade in salt. The wealth this gave Chichén was a major reason why it could dominate the Yucatán.

## 4 Ek-Balam

In 1998 excavations revealed some of the finest examples of Mayan sculpture at these ruins, on the giant temple-mound known as the Acropolis. Most spectacular is El Trono (The Throne), a temple entrance believed to be the tomb of Ukit-Kan-Lek-Tok, a ruler around AD 800. Nearby is an intricate mass of finely carved figures. The rest of the Acropolis is a multi-level palace *(see also p38)*. *Map F2 • www.inah.gob.mx • 8am–5pm daily • Adm (free Sun)*

## 5 Balankanché Caves

This great labyrinthine complex of caves extends several miles under the Yucatán forest. Caves were sacred for the ancient Maya and, in one spectacular chamber, the sanctuary, remains were found of over 100 ritual incense burners. The compulsory tour ends in a magical chamber with a perfectly still pool, in which the cave bottom seen through the water is a mirror image of the roof. *Map E3 • 9am–4pm daily • Adm*

## 6 Chichén Itzá

The most famous and awe-inspiring of all the great ancient Mayan cities, and the one with the most spine-tingling images of war and sacrifice. The great pyramid of El Castillo, the giant Ball Court, the Sacred Cenote, and the Temple of the Warriors are all must-sees *(see pp22–5)*.

## 7 Río Lagartos

This quiet village on the remote north coast is at the head of over 20 km (12 miles) of mangrove lagoon and mud flats, with the Yucatán's largest colonies of flamingos and a dazzling variety of other birds. Local boatmen provide good-value tours *(see also pp49 & 55)*. *Map F1*

Chichén Itzá

San Felipe

## 8 San Felipe

West of Río Lagartos, this village is smaller and has a superb, usually near-empty beach on the sandbar across the lagoon, facing the opal waters of the Gulf of Mexico. Village boatmen will ferry you to and from the beach, and also offer flamingo tours. From the village there are fabulous sunsets *(see also pp49 & 55)*. *Map E1*

## 9 Izamal

The most unaltered Spanish colonial city in the Yucatán, known as the *ciudad dorada* or "Golden City" because of the color of its buildings, is centered on the huge monastery of San Antonio, begun in 1549 as the headquarters of the Franciscan friars in Yucatán and the shrine of Our Lady of Izamal, the region's patron. A short walk away are the remains of three pyramids, traces of a much older Mayan city *(see also pp40 & 42)*. *Map D2*

## 10 Telchac and Uaymitún

Far west of San Felipe, a road joins the coast to run along it through quiet fishing villages. Seaward, there are endless, often empty, Gulf Coast beaches, while on the landward side is a lagoon full of birds. Telchac is a fishing harbor with fine beaches and a few low-key restaurants and cheap hotels. At Uaymitún there is a free observation tower for bird-watching in the lagoon *(see also p49)*. *Map C/D2*

## A Two-Day Tour

### Day One

Stay the night in Valladolid or, better, the little town of Pisté just outside **Chichén Itzá**, and get to the ruins as early as possible. Once inside, tackle the climb up the Castillo for an overview of the ancient city in all its majesty. Spend at least three hours around Chichén, then regain your strength with lunch at the charming **Las Mestizas** in Pisté *(see p103)*.

In the afternoon, make a choice: if you're interested in the ancient Maya, go up to **Ek-Balam**, or head into **Valladolid** for a wander around its plaza, San Bernardino monastery, and the dramatic town cenote. Before it's too late in the day, head north to Río Lagartos (104 km/65 miles) to book a flamingo tour for the next morning. Stay at the **Hotel San Felipe** in San Felipe *(see p131)*.

### Day Two

The flamingos are best seen early, so you'll need to be off around 7am. A 2- or 4-hour tour takes you into an exuberant, rare natural world, through broad lagoons and narrow creeks. Afterward, for lunch, have a ceviche at Isla Contoy on the waterfront, or head down to **Tizimín** for steaks at the **Tres Reyes** *(see p103)* on its broad Colonial square.

From Tizimín, turn westward through miles and miles of cattle ranches to reach **Izamal**. Here you can look out on the town from the monastery's arcaded courtyard. The town's golden colors are especially lovely in the warm, early evening light.

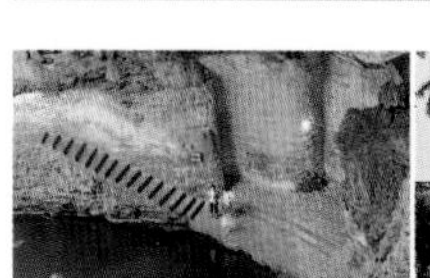

Left **Ikkil Cenote** Center **Tizimín** Right **Aké**

# TOP 10 Best of the Rest

### 1 Ikkil Cenote

A huge, circular pit filled with a beautiful underground pool – now the center of a private nature park. You can swim in the cenote pool and dine in the restaurant up above it. *Highway 180, 3 km (2 miles) E of Chichén Itzá • Map E3 • 9am–6pm daily • Adm*

### 2 Tihosuco

This remote village 50 km (30 miles) south of Valladolid was where the great Mayan revolt of the Caste War began *(see p37)*; it still bears the battle scars. A small museum tells the whole story. *Map E4 • Museum: 10am–5pm Tue–Sun • Adm*

### 3 Yaxcabá

An ultra-sleepy little town in the woods that surprises with a very imposing 18th-century church, with a unique three-tower façade and a beautifully carved wooden altarpiece. *Map D3*

### 4 Calotmul

Between Valladolid and Tizimín, this is another hot country town that has a fine church (1749) with a magnificently ornate Baroque altarpiece. *Map F2*

### 5 Tizimín

The hub of Yucatán's "cattle country" is a market town where tourism usually goes unnoticed. At its center are two spacious squares, divided by the massive walls of two Spanish monasteries *(see p40)*. *Map F2*

### 6 El Cuyo

At the end of a lonely road through savanna grass, forest, and sand flats, this tiny fishing village is a place to escape the crowds and sample miles of Gulf coast beaches *(see p55)*. *Map F1*

### 7 Bocas de Dzilam

This vast area of uninhabited mangroves west of San Felipe is remote and wild. There are no regular tours, but boatmen in San Felipe or Dzilam may offer a trip. *Map D1*

### 8 El Bajo and Santa Clara

Alongside the north coast road is a long, narrow sand-spit island, El Bajo, with deserted, coconut-palm shaded beaches. In the tiny village of Santa Clara you can find boatmen offering occasional trips to the island. *Map D1*

### 9 Aké

This ruined city west of Izamal is a mystery, as its drum-shaped columns and ramp-like stairways are unlike other Mayan buildings. The local church was built on an ancient pyramid *(see p39)*. *Map C2 • www.mayayucatan.com.mx • 8am–5pm daily • Adm*

### 10 Xcambó

The atmospheric ruins of a coastal Mayan town, probably an outlying Dzibilchaltún settlement. There are great sea views from the top of its main pyramid. *Map C2 • www.mayayucatan.com.mx • 8am–5pm daily • Adm*

Left **Valladolid's Main Plaza** Right **Aguilar Bike Hire**

# Top 10 Shops, Markets, and Tours

### 1 Valladolid's Main Plaza

Mayan women from the surrounding villages display their beautifully bright *huípiles* (traditional dresses) and other embroidery on the railings of the Parque Principal. *Map E3*

### 2 Valladolid Craft Market and Bazaar

Valladolid's semi-official handicrafts market has some very fine embroidery, as well as more production-line goods. The nearby bazaar is a quirky collection of shops around a food court *(see p103)*. *Mercado de Artesanías Calle 39, corner of Calle 44 • Map E3*

### 3 Yalat, Valladolid

On Valladolid's central plaza, Yalat offers embroidered clothes, jewelry, Mexican chocolate, and bath scrubs made from sisal fibre. *Cnr of Calle 39 and Calle 40 • Map E3*

### 4 Aguilar Bike Hire, Valladolid

From his ramshackle shop, former baseball player Antonio "Negro" Aguilar provides information, sells sports goods, and rents out cheap rooms and bikes at low rates. *Calle 44, between Calle 39 and Calle 41 • Map E3*

### 5 Handicrafts Market, Chichén Itzá

Around the Chichén visitor center there is almost a mall of handicrafts stalls, some run by Maya selling their own embroidery, hammocks, and wood carvings. *Map E3*

### 6 Market, Tizimín

Not a place to find souvenirs but a real, bustling country town market, with spectacular fruit and produce and household goods. *Map F2 • daily 8am–5pm*

### 7 Flamingo Tours, Río Lagartos

The best local boatmen's co-operative has a kiosk on the waterfront, just left of where the Tizimín road runs out. They work with the nature reserve and have good boats and experienced guides *(see p49)*. *Map F1 • (986) 862 0158*

### 8 San Felipe Tours

The boatmen's cooperative here is a bit less organized but also has a waterfront hut, in San Felipe village. Rates are similar to those in Río Lagartos, but boatmen here will be more ready to take you to the Bocas de Dzilam *(opposite)* and Río Lagartos lagoon *(see p49)*.

### 9 Hecho a Mano, Izamal

A pretty little shop with a more carefully selected display of handmade folk art than the markets, and striking photographs of Yucatecan scenes. *Calle 31, No.308, by the Town Hall • Map D2*

### 10 Market, Izamal

Izamal's market, just below the monastery, is a lively mix of souvenirs, handicrafts, and busy little cafés. *Calle 31/Calle 32* *Map D2 • daily 8am–5pm*

Left **La Chispa** Right **Hotel María de la Luz**

# Top 10 Drinking and Entertainment Spots

## 1 La Chispa, Valladolid

A surprisingly stylish, youth-oriented bar-restaurant with smartly designed metallic fittings around the patio of an old colonial house. *Calle 41, between Calle 42 and Calle 44 • Map E3 • $$*

## 2 La de Michoacán, Valladolid

Near the Chispa, this simple combination café, bakery, and ice-cream stand is a backpackers' favorite, and offers fresh juices and bargain snacks. *Calle 41, between Calle 42 and Calle 44 • Map E3 • $*

## 3 Sunday Concerts, Valladolid

Like many Yucatán towns, Valladolid puts on entertainment for free – the town band gives a concert every Sunday night in the square, with a musical menu that runs from rumbas and boleros to classic jazz. *Parque Principal • Map E3 • From 7:30pm Sun*

## 4 Hotel María de la Luz, Valladolid

This hotel has a big, well-shaded terrace on the Parque Principal, with very comfortable seats – ideal for lazy lounging while keeping an eye on all the movement in the square. *Calle 42 • Map E3 • $$*

## 5 Yepez II, Valladolid

This open-air restaurant and bar is lively on weekend afternoons, serving tasty tacos and other snacks. Live bands start after 9:30pm. *Calle 41, between Calle 38 and Calle 40 • Map E3 • $$*

## 6 Lonchería Fabiola, Pisté

The cheapest refreshment stops in Pisté are the budget *loncherías* (basic restaurants), such as this one on the village plaza, with outside tables for watching village life. *Map E3 • $*

## 7 Bar La Conchita, El Cuyo

A rumbustious village bar with a salsa soundtrack. The men of El Cuyo go out to fish before dawn, and when they come back many spend much of the day by the beach at La Conchita, which serves up wonderful grilled fish. *Map F1 • To about 7:30pm daily • $*

## 8 La Torreja, Río Lagartos

Friendly bar-restaurant with cool beers, great *ceviches* (raw fish salad, marinated in lime) and other Yucatecan snacks, and a fine view of the placid lagoon waters. *Opposite the Flamingo Tours kiosk • Map F1 • $*

## 9 Market Bars, Izamal

Several cafés and *loncherías* here share an outside terrace, a fine vantage point on the monastery and town life. Some serve beer, some only soft drinks to go with their snacks. *Calle 31, by Calle 32 • Map D2 • $*

## 10 Moctezuma ("Dos Barriles"), Chicxulub Puerto

This restaurant-bar is popular in the late afternoon with locals, who come for fresh *ceviche*, washed down with beer. *One block east of the plaza • Map C2 • $$*

*For the Top Ten Yucatecan dishes and snacks* **see pp68–9**

**Price Categories**
For a three-course meal for one with a beer of soda (or equivalent meal), taxes and extra charges.

| | |
|---|---|
| $ | under $5 |
| $$ | $5–$10 |
| $$$ | $10–$20 |
| $$$$ | $20–$35 |
| $$$$$ | over $35 |

Left **El Mesón del Marqués** Right **El Mexicano**

# TOP 10 Places to Eat

### 1 El Mesón del Marqués, Valladolid

Valladolid's foremost hotel also has its most distinguished restaurant, with tables around a plant-filled patio. Its versions of local specialties like *pollo oriental de Valladolid (see p68)* are definitive. *Calle 39, on Parque Principal • Map E3 • (985) 856 3042 • $$*

### 2 Cocinas Económicas, Valladolid

Around the bazaar on the square *(see p101)* there's a line of self-service food counters. Noisy, with lots of atmosphere, this is a great place for breakfast, and for local snacks. *Calle 39, on Parque Principal • Map E3 • No credit cards • $–$$*

### 3 El Mexicano, Valladolid

The restaurant in the Quinta Regia hotel *(see p131)* is cool and pretty. Its menu makes use of fresh local ingredients, including produce from the hotel garden. *Calle 40, No.160A, between Calle 27 and Calle 29 • (985) 856 3472 • $$*

### 4 Chaya's Natural Café, Ek-Balam

The restaurant at Genesis Retreat *(see p126)* is open to non-guests in the afternoon, but the crepes and chocolate-chili cookies make it worth a visit. *Off the northeast corner of the town plaza • Map F2 • $$$*

### 5 Las Mestizas, Pisté

Las Mestizas is the prettiest of the restaurants along the main road in Pisté, with the most charming service. It dishes up a delicious *sopa de lima (see p68)*. *Map E3 • No credit cards • $$*

### 6 Tres Reyes, Tizimín

Tizimín is the Yucatán's cattle capital, and so its best restaurant's specialty is steak, often cooked in thin strips (*arracheras*). *Calle 52, corner of Calle 53 • Map F2 • (986) 863 2106 • No credit cards • $$$*

### 7 Restaurante Isla Contoy, Río Lagartos

Under a drooping palm roof on a jetty, this place has a water-front feel and great seafood cocktails full of lime and coriander. *Map F1 • (986) 862 0000 • No credit cards • $*

### 8 Restaurante Vaselina, San Felipe

A big, unfussy, barn-like place on the seafront with plain tables where you can try wonderfully fresh, fat shrimp, octopus, and conch. *Map E1 • No credit cards • $$*

### 9 Kinich, Izamal

In a lush garden, this restaurant (open for lunch only) has a very high reputation for classic Yucatecan food, such as *poc-chuc (see p70)*. *Calle 27, No.299, between Calle 28 and Calle 30 • Map D2 • (988) 954 0489 • $$$*

### 10 Restaurante El Toro, Izamal

On a square near the monastery is this friendly little restaurant, with tasty Yucatecan dishes and tacos. *Plazuela 2 de Abril • Map D2 • No credit cards • $*

***Note:** Unless otherwise stated, all restaurants serve vegetarian meals; phone numbers are listed only where appropriate*

Left **Cafés, Mérida** Right **Mayapán**

# The West

NOWHERE IS THE FLAVOR OF THE YUCATÁN *more intense than in the west, around its historic capital, Mérida. In these parts, there is an extraordinary density of Mayan relics, and although they may not match the awesome power of Chichén Itzá, sites such as Uxmal show the architecture of the Maya at its most elegant. Beyond the main sights are stretches of wilderness, hidden lagoons, and small towns dripping with bougainvillea and hibiscus.*

Left **Chelem** Right **Warrior statue, Ticul**

## Top Ten Sights

1. Mérida
2. Celestún
3. Dzibilchaltún
4. Progreso
5. Uxmal
6. Kabah
7. Sayil
8. Labná
9. Loltún Caves
10. Campeche

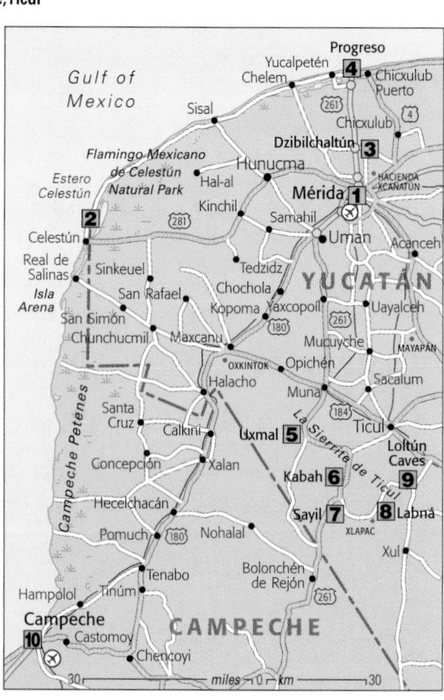

**Church, Ticul**


Chelem, Ticul, and Mayapán are covered on p108

## 1 Mérida

Perhaps the most seductive of all the colonial cities in Mexico. Elegant architecture, shady patios, great markets, a distinct friendliness, the soft music of *boleros* and the *jarana* heard in free concerts in 16th-century squares, and fiestas enjoyed by all ages every Sunday – the town's appeal is plentiful and varied *(see pp26–7)*.

## 2 Celestún

Just north of this fishing village is a silent, wild, watery expanse of mangrove lagoon that provides a breeding ground for great flocks of pink flamingos and ibises, egrets, and blue herons. Boat tours from the village are very popular (the lagoon can get rather crowded at times). But if you stay over in Celestún after the tours have gone back to Mérida, you will find a beautifully tranquil village, with a soft white beach, laid-back restaurants and hotels, and fabulous sunsets. *Map A2 • Tours from Celestún Embarcadero: 6am–5pm daily • Adm*

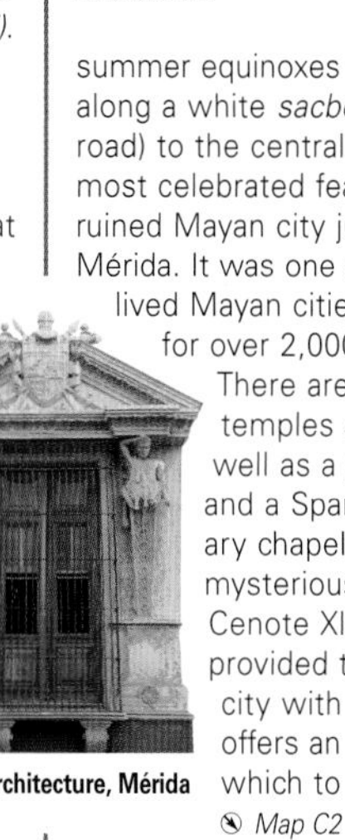

Colonial architecture, Mérida

## 3 Dzibilchaltún

The Temple of the Seven Dolls, through which the sun strikes at dawn on spring and summer equinoxes to run straight along a white *sacbé* (rough cast road) to the central plaza, is the most celebrated feature of this ruined Mayan city just north of Mérida. It was one of the longest-lived Mayan cities, occupied for over 2,000 years.

There are additional temples at the site, as well as a grand Palacio and a Spanish missionary chapel. The huge, mysterious pool – Cenote Xlacah – which provided the ancient city with water, now offers an idyllic place in which to cool off. *Map C2 • Cenote Xlacah: 8am–5pm daily • Adm Mon–Fri*

Dzibilchaltún

## 4 Progreso

Mérida's port and favorite beach town is a place to get close to ordinary Yucatecan life. The harbor is stuck at the end of a long (6-km/4-mile) pier, and so the shallow waters around the beach remain blissfully tranquil. Until the weekend, that is, when Meridanos spill out onto the sand and into the warm blue waters. There are excellent fish restaurants along the seafront, too, with big, convivial outside terraces for socializing *(see also p45)*.

Progreso's beach and long stone pier

Uxmal

## 5 Uxmal

With the elegant lines of the Nunnery Quadrangle and towering mass of the Pyramid of the Magician, Uxmal is not only one of the most beautiful of ancient Mayan cities but also one of the greatest sights in the Americas *(see pp28–9)*.

## 6 Kabah

This site was the second most important of the Puuc Cities *(see p31)* after Uxmal, and an imposing arch on its west side marks the start of the *sacbé* road *(see p88)* that linked it to its larger ally. Its Codz Poop or "Palace of Masks" is the most extravagant example of Mayan carving: the extraordinary façade is covered with 250 faces of the long-nosed rain-god Chac. The Palacio and Temple of the Columns are other classics of refined Puuc architecture. *Map C4 • 8am–5pm daily*

## 7 Sayil

Of all the Puuc Cities, Sayil is the one that gives the strongest sense of the wealth of its ancient inhabitants. Its hub is the magnificent Palacio, an opulent complex sweeping up through three levels and over 90 chambers, with an architectural refinement that recalls the buildings of Ancient Greece. It housed over 350 people, from lords to servants, and had its own exclusive water supply. *Map C4 • 8am–5pm daily • Adm*

Kabah

Snake head, Labná

## 8 Labná

The Arch of Labná (wonderfully drawn by Frederick Catherwood, *see box*) exemplifies the sophistication of Puuc architecture. Nearby, the town's Palacio is only slightly smaller than Sayil's, and was divided into seven patios – the part to the left was the home of the lords of Labná, the patios to the right (east) were for servants. The setting is especially lovely, in tranquil woods full of birds. *Map C4 • 8am–5pm daily • Adm*

## 9 Loltún Caves

This vast cave complex is both a stunning natural phenomenon and ancient Mayan site. It has been occupied by humans longer than anywhere else in the Yucatán, from remote prehistory right up until the 19th century. The ancient Maya lived here, mined the caves, and used them for rituals. Guided tours take you



*For more about the Mayan ruins* **see pp38–9**

Campeche

through 2 km (1.5 miles) of caves, but the network extends much further. The rock formations are awe-inspiring, and a special feature of Loltún is its strange changes of temperature, from fierce heat to chilly breezes *(see also p53)*. *Map C4 • Tours 8–11am and 2–4pm Mon–Sat, 8–11am Sun • Adm*

### 10 Campeche

A Spanish colonial walled city that retains a charming, old-world feel. The 17th-century ramparts and bastions were built to defend it against pirates. The streets within are lined with delicately colored old houses featuring patios and iron-grilled windows. A museum, housed in an old Spanish fort, contains jade funeral masks and other fine relics from the recently excavated site at Calakmul *(see pp34–5)*.

**Stephens and Catherwood**

The existence of ancient Mayan civilization was brought to the world's attention by American traveler John Lloyd Stephens (1805–52) and English artist Frederick Catherwood (1799–1854). Traveling together in 1839–42, they provided the first full descriptions and drawings of Chichén Itzá and Uxmal, and are credited with the discovery of Kabah and Sayil, among others.

## A Day in the Puuc Hills

### Morning

Leave **Mérida** early in a rental car. Beyond the suburb of Umán, where you turn onto Highway 261, traffic thins out, and you'll have an easy drive through woods and a few placid villages.

Stop at **Yaxcopoíl** *(see p108)* for a quick tour of the hacienda, a remarkable vision of early 20th-century aristocratic life in the Yucatán. Beyond Muna the road enters the Puuc Hills, before dropping down again to **Uxmal**. Devote at least two hours to this site, keeping an eye out for iguanas as well as the architecture.

Recoup your energies by heading back up the road a little to the **Restaurante Hal-Tun** *(see p111)*, for *sopa de lima* on the roadside terrace.

### Afternoon

Head straight for **Kabah** to marvel at the monsters of the Codz Poop.

Further south, the "Puuc Route" turns off the main Highway 261 onto a lovely woodland road, with only a few other tourists, combis, tricycle carts, and the birds for company. Along the way are stop-offs at the Puuc sites of **Sayil,Xlapak** *(see p39)*, and **Labná**. At the end of the road, descend into the netherworld of **Loltún**, refreshing yourself afterward in its café.

Go down to Oxcutzcab, and turn left for **Ticul** *(p108)*. Dine on *poc-chuc* at **Los Almendros** *(p111)* and take a stroll around the plaza to soak up some Yucatán country life before you drive back to Mérida.

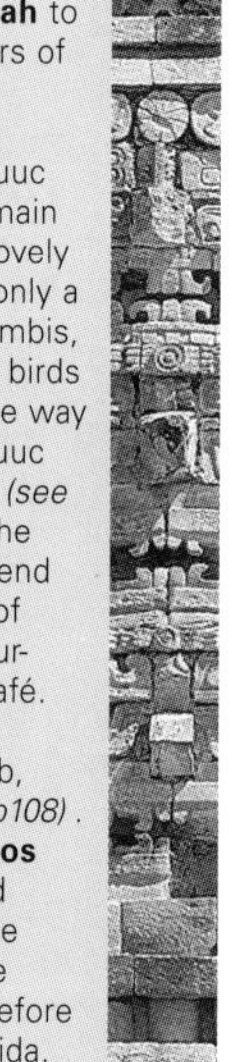

*For more about Dzibilchaltún, Kabah, Sayil, and Labná, visit www.inah.gob.mx*

Left **Chelem** Center **Ticul** Right **Mayapán**

# TOP 10 Best of the Rest

**1 Chelem and Yucalpetén**
Just west of Progreso, on the other side of a gap in the coastal sand bar, these easy-going villages have long, almost empty beaches. They're popular for windsurfing. *Map C2*

**2 Oxkintok**
This ancient Mayan city has a Satunsat, or "Labyrinth" pyramid, containing a strange, dark maze, possibly built as an entrance to the Underworld that only the Lord of Oxkintok could use. *Map B3 • 8am–5pm daily • Adm*

**3 Yaxcopoíl Hacienda**
Of all the restored haciendas in the Yucatán, this one, with its crumbling, ornate main house and factory buildings, gives the best feel of life here when *henequen* or "green gold" *(see p37)* dominated the state. *Map C3 • 8am–6pm Mon–Sat, 9am–1pm Sun • Adm*

**4 Cenotes**
The cenotes and underwater rivers in western Yucatán are far less well explored than those around Tulum *(see pp18–19)*. Snorkeling and diving trips are beginning to be organized from Mérida; Yucatán Trails agency *(see p124)* can book tours.

**5 Xlapak**
The smallest Puuc site is as attractive for the undisturbed woodland walk as for its ruins. The little Palacio has intricate Puuc carving *(see p31)*. *Map C4 • www.inah.gob.mx • 8am–5pm daily • Adm*

**6 Ticul**
One of the most charming of Yucatán's country towns *(see also p41)*, and an enjoyable base in the Puuc region, Ticul is also a historic center for ceramics. *Map C4*

**7 Acanceh**
On one side of the square of this remarkable little town is an 18th-century church, while on another is a very ancient Mayan pyramid, perhaps begun around 300 BC *(see pp40–41)*. *Map C3*

**8 Mayapán**
The last big Mayan city, and one that dominated the Yucatán for 200 years after 1200. Its buildings often "mimic" Chichén Itzá and have well-preserved frescoes. *Map C3 • www.inah.gob.mx • 8am–5pm daily • Adm*

**9 The Campeche Petenes**
This mangrove and forest wilderness is home to a wide range of wildlife such as pumas and turtles. Trips can be arranged from Campeche or the village of Isla Arena *(see p49)*. *Map A4*

**10 Edzná**
A Mayan city as spectacular as Chichén Itzá. The "Building of the Five Stories" is one of the largest Mayan palaces *(see also p35)*. *Map B5 • www.inah.gob.mx • 8am–5pm daily • Adm*

Left **Mexicanísimo, Mérida** Center **Guayaberas Jack, Mérida** Right **Arte Maya, Ticul**

# TOP 10 Places to Shop

### 1 Mérida Market
One of the world's greatest markets, a labyrinth of alleys and stalls selling everything imaginable – fish, fruit, a dazzling variety of chilies, rows of *huípil* dresses, sandals, and hats. *Calle 65, between Calle 54 and Calle 58 • Map C2*

### 2 Bazar de Artesanías Craft Market, Mérida
This semi-official handicrafts market is packed with stalls selling every kind of Yucatecan and Mexican craft work, some of it excellent, some rather tatty. *Calle 67, by corner of Calle 56 • Map C2*

### 3 Casa de Artesanías, Mérida
The Yucatán state handicrafts store has high-quality local work, with many beautiful, usable things especially in textiles, basketware, and wood. *Calle 63, No.503, between Calle 64 and Calle 66 • Map C2*

### 4 Hamacas Aguacate, Mérida
Only hammocks, of every size and color, and all of fine quality. The staff speak some English and take great care to find out just what you want. *Calle 73, by Calle 58 • Map C2*

### 5 El Sombrero Popular, Mérida
A little hat shop opposite the market, with a very friendly owner who will show you piles of handmade panamas in all sorts of styles and sizes. *Calle 65, between Calle 58 and Calle 60 • Map C2*

### 6 Maya Chuy, Mérida
This charming shop away from Mérida's crowded shopping streets is the outlet of a women's embroidery cooperative. Blouses, mats, and other items are beautifully, individually made. *Calle 60, between Calle 47 and Calle 49 • Map C2*

### 7 Mexicanísimo, Mérida
Innovative store that sells lightweight clothes for men and women in original, modern designs, using Mexican cottons and other traditional materials. *Parque Hidalgo Calle 60, between Calle 59 and Calle 61 • Map C2*

### 8 Guayaberas Jack, Mérida
The *guayabera* shirt-jacket is the smartest thing for gentlemen to wear in tropical Mérida. This long-established shop sells only *guayaberas*, and can make them to measure. *Calle 59, No.507, between Calle 60 and Calle 62 • Map C2*

### 9 Arte Maya, Ticul
Ticul produces huge quantities of ceramics. This family-run store stands out for the owners' skills and careful use of traditional and even ancient Mayan techniques. *Calle 23, No.301 • Map C4*

### 10 Casa de Artesanías Tukulná, Campeche
Campeche's state handicrafts store has ceramics, embroidery, basketwork, and many other top quality items that are beautifully displayed. *Calle 10, No.333, between Calle 59 and Calle 61 • Map A5*

Left **Casa Vieja** Center **La Parranda** Right **Flamingos**

# TOP 10 Drinking and Entertainment Spots

**1 Pancho's, Mérida**
The liveliest, most enjoyable bar-restaurant and dance club in central Mérida has Mexican bandit decor, welcoming staff, and a tiny, buzzing open-air dance floor *(see p61)*. *Calle 59, No.509, between Calle 60 and Calle 62 • Map C2 • $$*

**2 Dulcería y Sorbetería El Colón, Mérida**
Choose from a huge array of fruit-flavored sorbets and ice creams at this plaza-front parlor. A popular order is a *champola*, scoops of fruit ice served in a tall glass with milk. *Calle 59, on the plaza • Map C2 • $*

**3 El Cumbanchero, Mérida**
The son of Buena Vista Social Club member Rubén González runs this small salsa bar. Live bands start around 10pm for older but very energetic dancers. *Paseo Montejo at Calle 39 • Map C2 • $*

**4 Las Brasas, Mérida**
The cooler nightlife in Mérida takes place on Paseo de Montejo, and this bar-restaurant has a great view of the paseo from a roof terrace. It has good snacks and a laid-back feel. *Paseo de Montejo 462, by Calle 37 • Map C2 • $$*

**5 La Parranda, Mérida**
At the weekend, when they put tables outside, this restaurant is an ideal spot for observing all the activity in Parque Hidalgo. Settle in with a drink, and try one of the great enchiladas or another of their Mexican classics. *Calle 59, No.502 Centro • Map C2 • (999) 928 1691 • $$*

**6 Jugos California, Mérida**
Fresh-juice stands are a wonderful local institution, and California wins the prize as the best in town. Watermelon, pineapples, papaya, and more are all waiting to be juiced. *Calle 63A, corner of Calle 58 • Map C2 • $*

**7 El Edén, Mérida**
A snug, out-of-the-way bar in the patios of an old house, with distinctly quirky decor of tangled wood and old furniture and lots of intimate corners. *Calle 55, between Calle 56 and Calle 58 • Map C2 • $$*

**8 Flamingos, Progreso**
One of Progreso's most enjoyable big terrace bar-restaurants, with tasty *ceviches (see p69)* to go with the beer. *Malecón, corner of Calle 22 • Map C2 • $$*

**9 Casa Vieja, Campeche**
Watch the sun set from the balcony of this Cuban restaurant-bar on Campeche's central square. Enjoy their minty Mojitos made with Cuban rum. *Calle 10 No.319, Altos on the plaza • Map A5 • $$*

**10 La Principal, Campeche**
Around the bandstand in the middle of Campeche's main square are the terrace tables of this café, with sandwiches and Mexican snacks as well as the necessary drinks. *Parque Principal • Map A5 • $*

**Price Categories**

For a three-course meal for one with a beer or soda (or equivalent meal), taxes and extra charges.

| | |
|---|---|
| $ | under $5 |
| $$ | $5–$10 |
| $$$ | $10–$20 |
| $$$$ | $20–$35 |
| $$$$$ | over $35 |

Left **Hacienda Ochil** Right **Los Almendros, Ticul**

# TOP 10 Places to Eat

### 1 Hacienda San José Cholul
Set in a colonial hacienda, this restaurant's biggest draw is the secluded garden. The service is also excellent. *Highway Tixkokob–Tekanto, km 30 • Map C2 • (999) 960 9033 • $$$$*

### 2 Casa de Piedra, Xcanatún
Another comfortable hacienda restaurant in a garden, Casa de Piedra combines local and Caribbean cooking with a few French touches *(see pp70–71)*. *Xcanatún, 12 km (7 miles) N of Mérida • Map C2 • (999) 941 0213 • $$$$$*

### 3 Amaro, Mérida
One of old Mérida's loveliest patios houses this relaxing restaurant, which has a half-vegetarian menu, including several dishes made with the special Yucatecan vegetable chaya. *Calle 59, No.507, between Calle 60 and Calle 62 • Map C2 • (999) 928 2451 • No credit cards • $$$*

### 4 El Marlin Azul, Mérida
*Ceviche* is the dish to order at this seafood restaurant but also try the shrimp fajitas. Go for lunch, as it closes at 4pm *(see p70)*. *Calle 62 No.488, between Calle 57 and Calle 59 • Map C2 • (999) 928 1606 • $$$*

### 5 El Principe Tutul-Xiu, Maní
Set under a giant palapa roof, this restaurant is busiest on Sundays, when families drive from Mérida to eat *poc-chuc*, *panuchos* and other Yucatecan staples. *Calle 26 No.208, between Calle 25 and Calle 27 • Map C4 • $$$*

### 6 La Palapa, Celestún
Automatic first choice in Celestún, an ideally comfortable beach terrace beneath a palapa roof, with succulent, coriander-rich platters of fish, shrimp, and octopus. *Calle 12, by corner of Calle 11 • Map A3 • (988) 916 2063 • $$$*

### 7 Hacienda Ochil
A restaurant in a restored hacienda, offering finely prepared traditional Yucatecan dishes on a delightful terrace. *Off Highway 261, signposted about 40 km (25 miles) from Mérida • Map C3 • (999) 910 6035 • $$$*

### 8 La Palapa del Lodge, Uxmal
Located opposite the ruins of Uxmal, this restaurant has a tropical garden, ethnic artworks, and fine local and international cuisine. *Antigua Carretera Mérida-Campeche km 78 • Map C4 • $$$*

### 9 Los Almendros, Ticul
This country restaurant is credited with almost reinventing traditional Yucatecan food for the outside world. Try the *pavo en relleno negro*, a great example of the rich flavors of local cooking *(see p71)*. *Calle 23, No.207, by Calle 26A • Map C4 • (997) 972 0021 • $$$*

### 10 Marganzo, Campeche
Bright and comfortable, this popular restaurant is an excellent place to sample the distinctive, sea-based cuisine of Campeche *(see p71)*. *Calle 8, No.265, between Calle 57 and Calle 59 • Map A5 • (981) 811 3895 • No credit cards • $$$*

***Note:** Unless otherwise stated, all restaurants serve vegetarian meals; phone numbers are listed only where appropriate*

# STREETSMART

Left **Insect coil and repellent** Right **Sian Ka'an reserve**

# Top 10 Planning Your Trip

### 1 Seasons

The Yucatán has a tropical weather pattern, with a dry season building up in heat from November to June, and a wet season from June to November. The months of September to November are when hurricanes are most possible. The peak seasons for vacation travel (and so for prices) are from mid-December to March, and July and August. The lowest prices are available in May and June, and October and November.

### 2 Passports and Visas

U.S. and Canadian citizens can officially enter Mexico with only their birth certificate or a certified copy of it, but in practice it's better to take a passport. Citizens of the UK, Ireland, other EU countries, Australia, and New Zealand must have a full passport to enter Mexico, but do not need visas for stays up to six months.

### 3 Currency

Mexican pesos and U.S. dollars are accepted in the Yucatán. Mexican banks are happy to change American dollars and, to a lesser extent, Canadian dollars, but other currencies can be very problematic and expensive to change. It is therefore best to take credit cards and U.S. dollars in cash or traveler's checks *(see p118)*.

### 4 Customs Regulations

There are few limits on the items that visitors can bring for their personal use, including up to 12 rolls of film or video cassettes. However, there are restrictions on the import of plants and perishable foods, and very strict restrictions on firearms, which can be confiscated without compensation.

### 5 Insurance

Take out a comprehensive travel insurance policy that covers cancellations, loss of baggage, theft, and all medical eventualities, including repatriation. If you intend to go scuba diving you may need additional cover, so check your policy carefully.

### 6 Packing

Despite the usual warmth in the Yucatán, it's useful to have a long-sleeved shirt and long trousers when you're exploring Mayan ruins and forests, to avoid sunburn, scratches, and bug bites. Other things that are cheaper or more easily obtained outside Mexico include film and snorkels, but excellent sunhats can be bought once you're here.

### 7 Health Precautions

There are no obligatory inoculations for travelers to Mexico, but as a precaution it's advisable to be immunized against typhoid, tetanus, polio, and hepatitis A. If you're heading into forest areas further south in Central America, consult your doctor about taking malaria pills. A basic first-aid kit would include bite cream, antiseptic wipes, and stomach remedies.

### 8 Insect Repellent

Bug repellent is a must anywhere near forests and mangroves, and you will have a better choice of products if you buy before you come to Mexico. The best types contain the common ingredient DEET. There are more natural alternatives that smell better, but unfortunately they're not as effective.

### 9 Electricity

Electricity operates on a 110 volt system, as in the U.S. and Canada, and with the same American-type flat-pin plugs. If you bring any 220–240 volt equipment, you will need a transformer and plug adaptor.

### 10 Special Interest Tours

If you plan activities such as scuba diving, cave diving, Sian Ka'an tours, and adventure trips on a fixed schedule, try to book trips as far ahead as possible, by e-mail or the Net. Many operators are small-scale and quickly fill up, especially in peak seasons.



Previous pages **La Madonna, Cancún** ***(see p82)***

Left **Aerocaribe poster** Center **Cancun Airport** Right **Ferry**

# TOP 10 Arriving in the Yucatán

### 1 International Airports

The main international airport for the Peninsula is 15 km (9 miles) south of Ciudad Cancún, near the southernmost point of Cancún Island. Cozumel and Mérida also have international connections. Flights from the U.S. and Canada are numerous. From the UK, unless you get a charter, expect a stop-off at at Mexico City or a U.S. airport en route.

### 2 Tourist Cards

All visitors must fill in a Mexican Tourist Card, which will be stamped with the length of your permitted stay, from 30 days to six months. Keep it with your passport, since it must be collected at check-in when you leave. If you need more than 30 days, explain this to the Immigration Officer or apply for an extension at the Mexican Immigration Office in Cancún.

### 3 Customs Checks

You must also fill in a customs form. If you go through the nothing-to-declare channel at the airport you will have to press a button on a machine. It randomly flashes either green (go straight ahead) or red (meaning your bag will be searched).

### 4 Changing Money at the Airport

There are exchange desks in the baggage hall, but they always give very bad rates. Change only the minimum you need to get into Cancún, then find a bank.

### 5 From Cancún Airport into Cancún

Van-sized *colectivo* buses are the most accessible means of public transport into town. They go along the Hotel Zone and into Ciudad Cancún, dropping each passenger at their hotel, and the full journey takes an hour. Airport taxis are hard to find. However, when you're leaving, any Cancún city cab can take you to the airport *(see p116)*.

### 6 From Cancún Airport to Other East Coast Resorts

A Riviera bus leaves for Puerto Morelos and Playa del Carmen almost hourly, 10:30am–7pm. There are also hourly *colectivos* 6am–6pm from outside Domestic Arrivals. An airport cab to Puerto Morelos or Playa will cost around $15. If you're going anywhere else on the coast, take the bus to Playa and go on from there.

### 7 Cozumel Airport

The island's airport is just north of San Miguel town. Official airport taxis and *colectivos* are the usual means of transportation.

### 8 Mérida Airport

Mérida airport is about 4 km (3 miles) southwest of the city center. *Colectivo* buses and airport taxis operate.

### 9 Driving from the U.S.

You will need a Tourist Card if you travel beyond the 20-km (12-mile) border zone and if you stay for more than 72 hours. You should also obtain Mexican insurance and a Temporary Import Permit for your vehicle, which is valid for six months. Allow five days or so to drive from the Texas border to the Yucatán.

### 10 Ferries from Florida

A car and passenger ferry service runs between Florida and the Yucatán, with regular sailings between Tampa and Progreso and Puerto Morelos. Each trip takes around 24 hours.

#### Directory

**Immigration Office**
*Cancún airport • (998) 886 0092 • 7am–7pm Mon–Fri*

**Airlines in Cancún**
*• Aeroméxico (998) 849 2222 • American Airlines (998) 886 0247, Toll free 01 800 904 6000 • Continental (998) 886 0006 • Iberia (998) 886 0243 • Click Mexicana (998) 881 9090*

**Ferries**
*• www.yucatanexpress.com*

Left **Taxi** Center **Cancún bus** Right **Passenger ferry**

# Top 10 Getting Around Tips

### 1 Internal Flights
Aerocaribe *(see p115)*, a Mexicana subsidiary, has the most routes in the Yucatán. Fares are quite high, so take advantage of the Mexipass discount system *(see p123)*. Low-cost airlines include Volaris (www.volaris.com.mx) and Interjet (www.interjet.com.mx).

### 2 Long-Distance Buses
Buses are the main form of transport for longer trips, unless you rent a car or fly. First-class buses are air-conditioned and run between main towns with only a few stops en route. Second-class buses stop more often and are cheaper.

### 3 Local Buses, Combis & Colectivos
Every city has a local bus service. Destinations are usually displayed on the windscreen, but in Cancún buses have route numbers (routes R-1 and R-2 run up and down the Hotel Zone and to Ciudad Cancún). *Combis*, also known as *colectivos*, are minibuses that serve the smaller districts.

### 4 Ferries to Isla Mujeres
Passenger ferries run from Puerto Juárez, just north of Cancún, about every half hour daily. Fast boats take 20 minutes and the fare is around $4. There are five car ferries daily from Punta Sam, north of Puerto Juárez (around $22 for a car and two people). Shuttle boats also run from points along Cancún beach.

### 5 Ferries to Cozumel
Passenger ferries run roughly every two hours between Playa del Carmen (984 871 5109, Calica 984 879 3113) and Cozumel. The trip takes 30 minutes. A Cozumel Shuttle runs from Playa Tortugas in Cancún. The car ferry from Puerto Morelos is infrequent and expensive.

### 6 Taxis
Mexican taxis do not have meters. Instead, there are officially set rates for each locality, with extra charges for longer journeys, which are usually posted up at bus stations and some taxi stands. In Cancún, the official rates are significantly higher for journeys to and from anywhere in the Hotel Zone than in Ciudad Cancún. In Cancún and on the coast agree the fare before you get in the cab, to avoid scams *(see p120)*.

### 7 Car Rental
A car is a huge advantage for getting to Mayan ruins and isolated beaches. There are plenty of rental offices on the Riviera, but if you are touring around the Yucatán it's best to rent in Mérida, where rates are lower *(see p123)*. To rent a car you need to be over 21 and have your driving license, passport, and a credit card. Jeeps are a popular choice.

### 8 Fuel and Tolls
Prices are usually higher than in the U.S. but lower than in Europe for both unleaded *(magna* or higher-grade premium) and diesel fuel. Gas stations are scarce in some areas *(see p120)*. There are two fast toll highways in the Yucatán, the 180-Cuota part of the way between Cancún and Mérida, and another stretch between Campeche and Champotón. Tolls are high ($25, Cancún–Mérida), so most drivers prefer the parallel old road (180–Libre).

### 9 Scooters, Golf Carts & Bikes
Scooters and golf carts are available for rent in many resorts. Cancún has a dedicated cycle track all along the Hotel Zone, and many hotels have bikes for guests' use. Isla Mujeres is ideal for cycling, as are Tulum and Valladolid.

### 10 On Foot
Old Yucatán towns like Mérida, Campeche, and Valladolid are compact, and strolling around is the best way to get to know them. Mechanized transport is only really essential in Cancún.

Left **Xcaret eco-park** Center **Local agency** Right **Maps and brochures**

# Top 10 Sources of Information

**1 Mexican Tourist Offices Abroad**
Official Mexican government tourist offices can provide information on major destinations. However, for more detailed and up-to-date information on specialist activities, small-scale hotels, ecotourism, and adventure tours, look at specialist independent agencies and websites.

**2 Tourist Offices in the Riviera**
The Cancún city tourist desks in the town hall and some shopping malls are staffed by students who can provide information on the main local attractions and services.

**3 Offices in Yucatán State & Campeche**
Mérida, Campeche, and Valladolid have tourist information offices.

**4 Websites**
A huge amount of information is available on the Internet *(see Directory)*. For diving, a search under "dive Mexico" will produce results.

**5 Free Magazines**
English-language freebies available in tourist offices, hotels, and restaurants include *Cancún Tips*, Cozumel's *Blue Guide*, *Yucatán Today* in Mérida, *Playa del Carmen*, and *Info-Tulum*. They contain maps, practical information, and sometimes discount coupons.

**6 English-Language Press**
*Miami Herald* produces a special edition for Cancún. *The News* is an English-language paper produced by the Mexico City daily *Novedades*.

**7 Local Travel Agencies**
These can be good for unusual local tours, diving, forest trips, and so on. Among the best are Mundaca Travel on Isla Mujeres and Yucatán Trails in Mérida. Internet cafés *(see p118)* are another good resource for finding out local info.

**8 Maps**
The free magazines have quite decent maps of their areas, but you will need to visit Mérida's Librería-Papelería Burrel for the best maps.

**9 Ecotourism**
Most ecotours are run by small-scale operators, which can be hard to locate. An essential resource is the Eco Travels in Mexico website. The Pronatura organization (www.pronatura.org.mx) is another useful resource. *(See also p124.)*

**10 Spanish-Language Press**
The *Diario de Yucatán* (a daily paper) is the main place to find out about any local fiestas and other events around the region. Town fiestas are usually given full-page ads.

## Directory

**Mexican Tourism Board**
- *U.S. and Canada; 1 800 44 MEXICO; www.visitmexico.com*
- *UK, (020) 7488 9392; http://mexicotravel.co.uk*

**Tourist Offices in the Yucatán**
- *Cancún: Cancún Town Hall, Av Tulum*
- *Playa del Carmen: Av Juárez, corner of Av 15*
- *Isla Mujeres:Av Rueda Medina 130*
- *Mérida:Teatro Peón Contreras, corner of Calle 60 and 57*
- *Campeche: Casa Seis, Parque Principal*
- *Valladolid: southeastern corner of town square*

**Websites**
- *www.cancun.com*
- *www.cozumelonline.com*
- *www.mexicanwave.com*
- *www.mexonline.com*
- *www2.planeta.com/madder/ecotravel/mexico (Eco Travels in Mexico)*

**Local agencies**
- *Mundaca Travel, Isla Mujeres (998) 877 0025, www.mundacatravel.com*
- *Yucatán Trails, Calle 62, No.482, Mérida (999) 928 2582*

**Maps**
- *Librería-Papelería Burrel, Calle 59 by Calle 60, Mérida*

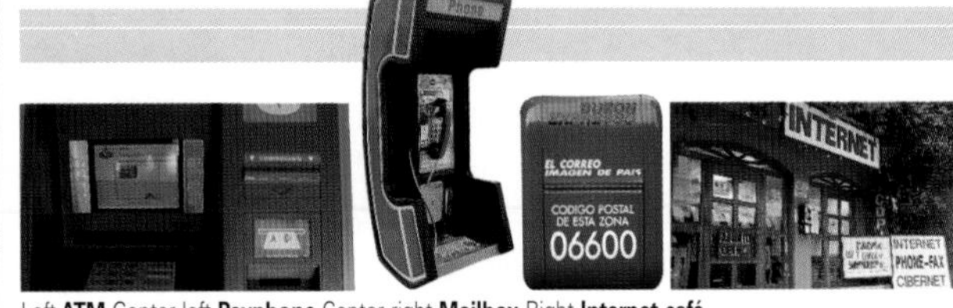


Left **ATM** Center left **Payphone** Center right **Mailbox** Right **Internet café**

# TOP 10 Banking and Communications

## 1 The Peso

Mexico's currency is the peso. There are coins for 1, 2, 5, and 10 pesos; and notes for 20, 50, 100, 200, 500, and 1000 pesos. There are also tiny coins for 10, 20, and 50 *centavos*, of which there are 100 to the peso. The usual symbol for the peso is the same as the dollar sign; prices quoted in U.S. dollars usually have the prefix US$ or suffix USD.

## 2 Using U.S. Dollars

Many Riviera businesses accept U.S. dollars as well as pesos, and a substantial number of visitors use only U.S. dollars during their trip. Hotel and restaurant listings in this book are given in price categories of U.S. dollars. Note, though, that U.S. dollar prices usually work out a bit higher than pesos. In the rest of the Yucatán, shops and businesses usually take pesos only.

## 3 Banks and ATMs

There are clusters of banks in the center of all main towns, but they can be hard to find in rural areas. Banks are generally open 8:30am–4pm Monday to Friday, and 9am–1pm Saturday, but some may not exchange money in the afternoons and on Saturdays. Most banks even in small towns now have ATMs, often the most economical way of obtaining cash *(see p120, no. 7)*.

## 4 Bureaux de Change

All tourist areas have many small exchange offices *(cambios)*, open daily. Exchange rates are usually almost as good as in the banks.

## 5 Credit Cards

MasterCard and VISA are widely accepted for larger purchases in shops, diving schools, and in hotels of mid-range level and above; Amex is less popular. Credit cards are virtually essential for car rentals, but some restaurants and smaller shops rarely accept them.

## 6 Telephones

White *lada* (long distance) payphones are easy to find in towns and tourist areas. Most take phone cards (*tarjeta de teléfonos)*, which can be bought for 30, 50, or 100 pesos at any shop with the blue and yellow Ladatel sign. In villages, there is always a *caseta,* or phone office, where the attendant dials the number for you and you take the call in a booth. Cellphones operate on the same band as in the USA (European mobiles do not usually work).

## 7 Phone Codes

To call anywhere in Mexico outside your local area, first dial 01, then the three-figure area code 998 for Cancún, or 999 for Mérida (given with all numbers in this guide) and then the number. Within the same area code, only dial the seven-figure number. To call outside Mexico, dial 00 followed by the country code. To call Mexico from abroad the code is 52. For long-distance calls to cell phones first dial 045.

## 8 Charges

Telephone charges are high in Mexico. Making an international call from your hotel room will be the most expensive of all – ask people to ring you from abroad whenever possible.

## 9 Mail

Post offices in towns generally open 9am–6pm Monday to Friday, and 9am–1pm Saturday. Small village branches may open only on weekday mornings. Stamps *(estampillas)* can also be bought at any shop with an Expendio de Estampillas sign. The Mexican mail service is very erratic, and postcards sent abroad can take weeks. For anything important, use the Mexpost courier service, available at main post offices.

## 10 Internet

Mexico has taken enthusiastically to the Internet, and Net cafés and easy-access Net shops are abundant, even in small towns. Most charge around $1–$2 an hour. E-mail is a far more reliable means of communication than the local postal service.

Left **Police station** Center **Ambulance** Right **Pharmacy sign**

# Top 10 Security and Health Tips

**1 Emergencies**
There are central phone numbers for all emergency services in Cancún (060) and Mérida (066), but in general it's better to call the local police directly, or the Red Cross in case of medical emergencies. In Cancún, the private, English-speaking clinics also have emergency ambulances.

**2 Swimming Safety**
Most waters around the Yucatán are placid, but take care on the eastern beaches of Isla Mujeres and Cozumel and on the surf beaches of Cancún Island, where seas are rougher and there can be a strong undertow. Check the warning flags (blue, safe; yellow, use caution; red, do not swim) before swimming. Several high-standard emergency facilities for divers are set along the Riviera, which all dive-masters will be in touch with.

**3 Personal Safety**
The Yucatán is a fairly tranquil place, but be wary of pickpocketing and other petty crime in Playa del Carmen. Cheaper *cabañas* on the north beach in Tulum are sometimes subject to break-ins at night.

**4 Begging**
There is a certain amount of street-hassling in Cancún, Playa, and Mérida, generally in the form of trying to sell you hammocks or other cheap craftwork rather than straight begging.

**5 Police Stations**
In most towns, the police station can always be found in the main square or next to the town hall. Cancún, Playa, Mérida, and some other towns have special Tourist Police (Policía Turística) units with English-speaking officers.

**6 Consulates**
There are U.S. consulates in Cancún, Cozumel, and Mérida. The UK and several other countries have consulates in Cancún.

**7 Women Travelers**
Lone women need to be careful in Playa del Carmen and parts of Cancún and Tulum. Avoid empty streets at night, lonely beaches around Playa, and obscure areas of Mayan sites.

**8 Health Services**
Visitors with full travel health insurance should turn to private clinics, such as the American Hospital in Cancún, or the Centro Médico de las Américas in Mérida, which have English-speaking staff. In small towns and country areas there are small public health centers *(centros de salud)* with emergency facilities.

**9 Pharmacies**
All Mexican towns and villages have pharmacies, often open 24 hours, which stock a huge range of medications.

**10 Water**
The quality of mains water has improved a lot, especially in Cancún. To be on the safe side, however, drink only bottled, purified water *(agua purificada)*, sold in grocery stores, supermarkets and pharmacies. Many hotels provide it for free, and most bars and restaurants use it to make ice.

## Directory

**Emergency Numbers**
*• Cancún Tourist Police 066 • Mérida Tourist Police 066 or (999) 983 1184*

**Red Cross Ambulances**
*• Cancún 065 or (998) 884 1616 • Mérida (999) 924 9813*

**Medical Clinics**
*• American Hospital Retorno Viento St No.15 Cancún (998) 884 6133*
*• Centro Médico de las Américas, C/54 No.365, nr Paseo Montejo, Mérida, (999) 926 2619*

**Consulates**
*• British (998) 881 0100*
*• Canadian (998) 883 33 60 • U.S. (Cancún) (998) 883 0272, (in Cozumel) (987) 872 4574, (Mérida) (999) 942 5700*

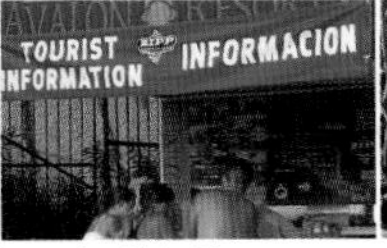

Left **Taxi** Center **Official tourist information** Right **Mangroves**

# Top 10 Things to Avoid

### 1 Taxi Scams

Taxis are subject to set fees (see p116). In Cancún, Playa del Carmen, and Tulum, though, cab drivers have a bad reputation for trying out exaggerated rates on all foreigners. In Cancún, also, the complicated official system, with different prices for the Hotel Zone and Ciudad Cancún, makes scams easier. Always agree a price before getting into the cab, and be firm in refusing any outrageous demands.

### 2 Topes – Speed Bumps

The main peculiarity of driving in Mexico is the *tope*, or speed bump, designed to make the streets safer for pedestrians and children. Very steep, they are usually signposted but can catch drivers unaware and cause damage to vehicles going at any speed above a crawl.

### 3 Running Low on Gas

Fuel stations are few and far between in many rural areas, so fill up whenever you can.

### 4 Fuel Station Scams

Occasionally, attendants start the pump with 30 or 50 pesos already on the gauge, or try to short-change tourists. To avoid these and any other scams, get out of the car and look straight at the pump. The attendant should then demonstrate that it is set at zero.

### 5 Driving at Night

Night falls very quickly in the tropics, and there is no lighting at all in country areas. *Topes*, potholes, and people on bicycles can rapidly become hazardous.

### 6 Bogus Information Booths

Along Avenida Tulum in Cancún, Quinta Avenida in Playa del Carmen, and some other locations there are any number of kiosks with eager staff buttonholing tourists and asking if they're looking for "information." They are actually selling specific tours or, at worst, timeshares. For less biased advice, stick to the official tourist offices *(see p117)*.

### 7 Running Low on Cash

At present there are no banks or ATMs on the southern Riviera between Playa del Carmen and Tulum, and only a few *cambio* offices, so plan accordingly. On Isla Mujeres and Cozumel, there are no money-exchange facilities outside Isla Town and San Miguel except in big hotels.

### 8 Crowds

The best-known Mayan ruins at Chichén Itzá and Tulum are very crowded around the middle of the day when most tour groups arrive, and especially on Sundays when admission is free. Therefore, try to get to them earlier in the day, after 8am, and forget the free Sundays. Lesser-known ruins in Yucatán State and Campeche are rarely subject to crowds.

### 9 Hurricanes

September to November are the months when hurricanes are most likely to hit. Mexico has extensive anti-hurricane precautions, and many buildings in Cancún and the Riviera have orange signs identifying them as an official Refugio Anticiclón, to be used as a public hurricane shelter when necessary.

### 10 Mangrove Mosquitoes

Mangroves are a breeding ground for mosquitoes. They are most active in the early evening, when they spread into neighboring areas – especially around Sian Ka'an, on Isla Holbox, and around watery areas and cenotes behind the coast near Puerto Morelos, Tankah, and some other points on the Riviera. Bug repellent can keep down their attacks, but the best way to avoid bites is just to stay away from those areas at dusk. The good news is that mosquitoes are not malarial in the Yucatán.

Left **Signs for disabled restrooms** Center **Airport transportation** Right **Wheelchair ramp**

# Top 10 Tips for the Disabled

## 1 Hotels

Some of the larger hotels and resort complexes in Cancún and Cozumel, especially those of Intercontinental, now have good wheelchair facilities. Hotels set in colonial-style patio buildings are difficult for access, but several have attractive ground-floor rooms. Check when booking.

## 2 Sidewalks

Most Cancún sidewalks now have wheelchair ramps at street junctions. Elsewhere, dips in the sidewalk provided for handcarts often do the job as well.

## 3 Transportation and Taxis

Public transportation provision for disabled people is poor, although there are wheelchair ramps and disabled toilets at Cancún Airport. Buses rarely have any special provision for wheelchairs or people with mobility problems, but this is often compensated for by the willingness of drivers to help disabled travelers. Many car rental agencies have larger vehicles: make clear what you need when booking.

## 4 Museums and Attractions

The main state museums, including the Anthropology Museum in Mérida, now have access ramps, and more are being provided (the Campeche fortress museums are entered by ramps in any case). Of the other attractions around the Yucatán, eco-parks and especially Xcaret *(see pp14–15)* are generally the easiest to visit and appreciate.

## 5 Mayan Sites

Larger Mayan ruins, such as Chichén Itzá and Uxmal, have (relatively) smooth walkways, and Cobá has a long forest path that is easy to negotiate at most points and is also great for birdwatching. Most ruins, though, have many steps and narrow, stony paths.

## 6 Island Ferries

The slow ferries to Isla Mujeres are much easier to get aboard with a wheelchair than the fast, enclosed boats, and the crews are very helpful. For Cozumel, there is no real alternative to the enclosed boats from Playa del Carmen, but staff, again, are helpful.

## 7 Swimming Pools

All hotels and public pools are now obliged to provide access and safety facilities for people with mobility problems, but upgrading amenities is proving a slow process.

## 8 Diving

Yucatek Divers in Playa del Carmen has a special program for disabled divers and can also arrange accommodation at the Casa Tucán hotel *(see p130)*.

## 9 Restrooms

Fully-adapted disabled restrooms are slowly being installed in official buildings (which include airports, state museums, some bus stations), but they are rarely found in private facilities. You are most likely to find good ones in Cancún and the main resort areas.

## 10 Further Information

The best way to find individual hotels that have disabled-friendly facilities is to search the Internet with "disabled" and then "Cancún," "Mérida," or any other location you are interested in. The websites for Mobility International USA and Access-Able also have many useful links.

### Directory

**Intercontinental Hotels**
*www.presidenteintercontinental.com*

**Yucatek Divers**
*Av 15 North, between C/2 & 4, Playa del Carmen • (984) 877 6026 or (984) 803 1363 • www.yucatek-divers.com*

**Mobility International USA**
*www.miusa.org*

**Access-Able**
*www.access-able.com*

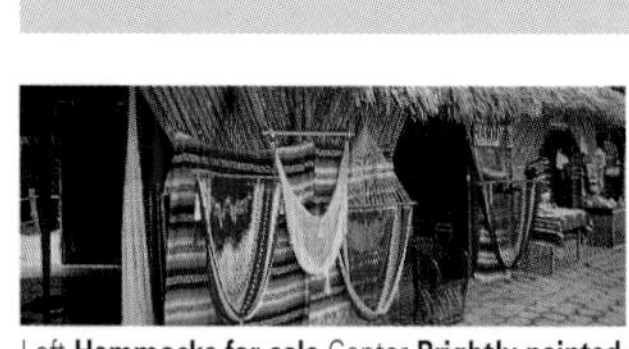

Left **Hammocks for sale** Center **Brightly painted ceramic ornament** Right **Panama hats**

# Top 10 Shopping Tips

### 1 Shop and Market Hours

Most shops open around 8:30am and close at 9pm, Monday to Saturday, with the more traditional ones closing for lunch from 1–3pm. Some local stores will always stay open for longer hours, and on Sundays, too. Sunday is a full shopping day in Valladolid and some other towns. Markets generally begin very early, before 8am, and close up by 2–3pm.

### 2 Bargaining and Discounts

Trying to haggle is fine in markets, especially for larger items, but should rarely be intensive or drawn-out. Many shops will offer discounts if you want to buy more than one of any article.

### 3 Official Handicrafts Stores

Mérida and Campeche have official handicrafts stores (Casas de Artesanías), which showcase all the traditional crafts of each state. They are a little more expensive than the norm, but provide an attractive overview of the work.

### 4 Gifts and Souvenirs

The Riviera is a huge souvenir repository: you'll find whole malls dedicated to souvenir items in Cancún and Playa del Carmen. The quality ranges from finely worked pieces to junk, so take time to browse. Favorite items include enamelled metal plaques and ornaments, Mayan-style wooden figures, brightly painted wooden parrots and toucans, and colorful coasters.

### 5 Jewelry

Gleaming jewelry stores aimed at cruise passengers and including some major names (Van Cleef & Arpels), are a specialty of Cozumel and, to a lesser extent, Isla Mujeres and Cancún. As well as a lot of fine silver, they have items made with local precious materials such as jade, amber, coral, and black obsidian. Prices are rising but are still tax-free and low. Playa del Carmen and Cancún have many stores showcasing ornate fine silver work from Taxco in central Mexico.

### 6 Cigars

Genuine Cuban Havana cigars are easy to obtain in Mexico, and are relatively cheap. All the Cancún malls contain specialist cigar stores with a full range of labels.

### 7 Tequila and Other Drinks

Sadly, tequila is now peculiarly expensive in its homeland. Take advantage of duty-free sales at Cancún airport, where there is an excellent selection. Cheaper and more local Yucatán specialties include several fine rums and *Xtabentún*, a sweet, herby, traditional Mayan drink made from honey.

### 8 Traditional Textiles

Fine embroidery of bright flower patterns on a plain white background is one of the foremost traditional products of the Yucatán, most often seen in the simple *huípil* dresses worn by Mayan women but also now used on other items like blouses, handkerchiefs, and tablecloths. Valladolid and Mérida are the best places to find good embroidery. Textiles from other parts of Mexico (Chiapas weaving, *sarape* blankets) are also available, but note that *sarapes*, especially, are often factory-made.

### 9 Hammocks

Hammocks vary a lot in quality. The cheap nylon ones sold by most street-sellers wear out quickly. The toughest ones are 100% cotton, and the specialist hammock shops in the market area in Mérida are by far the best places to look for one.

### 10 Panama Hats

Traditional Panamas make excellent, practical sunhats, and the good ones will regain their shape even after being rolled up for packing. Head for Mérida market and the small specialist hat shops nearby.

Left **Market produce** Right **Ecotourism sign**

# Top 10 Budget Tips

### 1 MexiPass Flight Discounts

The MexiPass system offers foreign visitors nearly 50% discount on Mexicana, AeroCaribe, and Aeroméxico domestic flights. Visitors traveling from North America need to book at least three internal flights to qualify for the discount; visitors from Europe need only two. You must book the MexiPass tickets at the same time as booking your entry flight (which can be with any airline).

### 2 Rent a Car in Mérida, not Cancún

Several small car-rental agencies in Mérida offer the best rates in the whole of the Yucatán – about 25% cheaper than in Cancún – especially for rentals of a week or more. Also, local agencies often look after their cars better than the bigger chains.

### 3 Go Low-Season

Hotel prices shoot up in the peak winter season, above all around Christmas and New Year, from mid-December to mid-January. To get the best combination of prices and weather, travel in May to June or late November to early December.

### 4 Use Pesos not Dollars

It may be convenient to pay in U.S. dollars, but you will save money in the long run if you change your money to pesos.

### 5 Discount Coupons

Local free magazines *(see p117)* often contain discount coupons for a whole range of local hotels, bars, restaurants, and other attractions, and you may also be given booklets of nothing but discount coupons for free drinks, meals, or park admissions. They may be annoying to carry around, but can save you significant amounts of money, especially in Cancún.

### 6 Free Sundays at Mayan Ruins

Admission to some Mexican national monuments, including some Mayan ruins, is free on Sundays. The hitch is that since everybody knows this, the popular ruins become very crowded – you may prefer to pay and go on a weekday.

### 7 Market Food and Snack Stands

There is always a row of simple restaurants in the food markets, offering traditional Yucatecan and Mexican food. These are the cheapest and often also the most atmospheric places to eat a full meal. You'll also find plenty of snack stands, offering tacos, tortas, peeled fruit, and other pleasures, which are very good value for money.

### 8 Share Costs on Ecotours

Boat trips to see flamingos in such places as Río Lagartos and Celestún, fishing trips, and tours to nature reserves like Sian Ka'an are often very expensive if you travel alone or as a couple; or there may be a minimum number to make a trip viable for the guide or tour operator. You can cut costs drastically and avoid disappointment by getting together a group of four to six to share a boat or bus.

### 9 Diving: Group and Multi-Dive Discounts

Most diving operators offer discounts for people diving in a group, or booking several dives at the same time. Many operators will also offer discount rates if you book in advance.

### 10 Two for One Drinks in Bars

Most bars on the Riviera offer a two-for-one deal on beers and other drinks for at least a few hours each night.

#### Directory

**MexiPass**
- *U.S. and Canada 1 800 531 7921*
- *UK 020 8492 0000*

**Mérida Car Hire**
- *Budget, Calle 60 No. 491 btwn 57 & 59, (999) 928 6759*
- *Alamo Aeropuerto, Highway Mérida-Uman, km 14.5, (999) 946 2255*

Left **Visiting Mayan ruins** Center **Snorkeling** Right **Dive shop**

# Top 10 Tours and Special Interests

### 1 Tours to Mayan Ruins

Many companies on the Riviera and in Mérida offer guided tours to the main Mayan sites, bookable through hotels and travel agents. Unfortunately, few allow more than an hour and a half on-site, and they often arrive all together at the hottest part of the day.

### 2 Licensed Guides at Mayan Ruins

Chichén Itzá, Uxmal, and Cobá have official, licensed guides who can show you round for an hourly fee. Able linguists, they are often highly informative. Guides at the smaller sites are less likely to be genuinely knowledgeable.

### 3 Air Tours

Aerosaab from Playa del Carmen and Isla Mujeres, and Cozumel-based Aerobanana offer light-plane trips, while Helitours offers helicopter tours over Cancún. *(See also p57.)*

### 4 City Tours

Mérida's Paseo Turístico bus leaves from Parque Santa Lucía four times daily Monday to Saturday, and twice on Sunday – the trip around Mérida's main sights takes about two hours. In Campeche, the Tranvía de la Ciudad runs from the Parque Principal, and another bus, El Guapo, also runs to the fortress-museums of San José and San Miguel.

### 5 Eco and Adventure Tours

Agencies in the Sian Ka'an reserve offer excellent day tours *(see pp20–21)*, and a growing number of companies specialize in nature and birdwatching trips.

### 6 Local Guides

Local boatmen in Río Lagartos and Celestún run trips to see the flamingos; while some fishermen in the Campeche Petenes can take you to places you'd never discover without local knowledge. In Puerto Morelos, American resident Goyo Morgan offers a popular "jungle adventure."

### 7 Cenote Tours

Cenote pools are a unique attraction of the Yucatán *(see pp52–3)*. Several specialists offer cenote tours, incorporating diving or snorkeling, especially around Tulum.

### 8 Diving

Dive shops abound on the Riviera, offering one-day "resort courses" for beginners, longer courses, and night dives.

### 9 Snorkel Tours

Cozumel is a great snorkeling area. Most dive centers and many small-boat operations offer snorkel tours to inshore reefs, often in glass-bottomed boats.

### 10 Fishing Trips

Specialist brokers and fishing lodges such as Boca Paila in Sian Ka'an are booked up far in advance. For more casual fishing, the best places to find captains with good boats are Isla Mujeres, Cozumel, Puerto Morelos, and the more rustic island of Holbox.

## Directory

**Air Tours**

*• Aerosaab, (984) 873 08 04, www.aerosaab.com*

**Ecotours and Guides**

*• Ecoturismo Yucatán, (999) 920 2772, www.ecoyuc.com.mx • Altournative, (984) 873 2036 • Best Day, (998) 881 1329 • Goyo's Jungle Tours, Puerto Morelos, www.goyosjungle.com*

**Diving, Snorkeling, and Cenote Tours**

*• Almost Heaven Adventures, Puerto Morelos, (998) 871 0230 • Aquatech-Villas de Rosa, Akumal, (984) 875 9020, www.cenotes.com • Cenote Dive Center, Tulum, (984) 871 2232, www.cenotedive.com • Mundaca Divers, Isla Mujeres, (998) 877 0607, www.mundacadivers.com • Phocea Caribe, Playa del Carmen, (984) 873 1210 • Aquaworld, Cancún, (998) 848 8300, www.aquaworld.com.mx • Yucatek Divers, Playa del Carmen, (984) 877 6026 or (984) 803 1363*

Left **Snack bar** Center **Restaurant** Right **Typical Mexican spices**

# Top 10 Eating and Drinking Tips

### 1 Restaurantes and Loncherías

Anywhere called a *restaurante* will usually be neater and more comfortable than a cheap, plastic-chaired *lonchería* (where you have your "lonch") or a *cocina económica* ("cheap kitchen"), the place to find no-nonsense local cooking.

### 2 Snack Stands

Mexicans are constant snackers. In every town, vendors offer tacos, *tortas* (filled bread rolls) and other *antojitos* (savory snacks), ice cream, or peeled fruit, from stalls or little handcarts. The most popular Yucatecan taco filling is *cochinita pibil* – spicy marinated pork. They're very cheap and don't usually have a bad effect on your stomach.

### 3 Juice Shops

The Yucatán's fruit is wonderfully fresh and juicy, from familiar types like watermelon to tropical mangos and mamey. Juice shops usually serve it three ways: as straight juice; a *licuado*, put through a blender with a little water; or an *agua*, diluted with water and ice. *(See also p71.)*

### 4 Breakfasts

The first meal of the day, before the heat rises, is an important part of the Mexican diet. Many restaurants offer hearty breakfasts, rich in eggs, beans, and sauces, followed by fresh fruit.

### 5 Meal Courses

Set meals do not fit easily with Mexican cooking. Some dishes are small and snack-like, others are big platters of mixed fish, seafood, and salads. There's no real obligation to have a first course, a second course, and a dessert. When Mexicans do have a first course, it's often a surprisingly heavy soup.

### 6 Spices and Fieryness

On most restaurant tables you'll find two little bowls of sauce. The red one is (relatively) gentle; the green one, made with *habanero* chilis, blows the head off the uninitiated. Apart from this, many local dishes are more fragrant than spicy.

### 7 Bills and Tipping

Most waiters will not bring you the check/bill (*la cuenta* or *la nota*) until you ask for it. It's normal to tip – the usual rate is about 10%, but on the Riviera waiters often expect the U.S. rate of 15%. Some restaurants now put a service charge – generally 10% – on the bill, in which case you're not expected to add more.

### 8 Beers and Wines

Mexico's beers are among its most successful exports. As well as internationally marketed brands (Corona, Dos Equis, Superior), the Yucatán has its own Montejo brewery, with a fine light beer (Montejo Especial) and a great ale, León Negra. It's more common to drink beer than wine in restaurants, as it goes better with local food. The quality of Mexican wines has been improving, but most restaurants have only a limited selection. Upscale restaurants have imported U.S., European, and Chilean wines, at high prices.

### 9 Tequila Tasting

Tequila comes from Jalisco in central Mexico, but is found everywhere in the Yucatán, and some Riviera bars specialize in tastings of the many different labels. *Blanco* is the youngest tequila; *reposado* is aged for up to 11 months; darker *añejo* is aged for up to five years. With so much being exported, though, the spirit has become expensive in Mexico itself.

### 10 Cantinas

The *cantina* is the most traditional type of Mexican bar. There used to be laws that women were not allowed inside, and that nobody should be able to see in. You can still find old-style *cantinas* with their secretive, screened doorways. However, there are now also new-model *cantinas* that are actually quite comfortable.

Left **Las Palapas** Center **Cabañas María del Mar** Right **Genesis Retreat**



# TOP 10 Cabaña Hotels

### 1 Shangri-La Caribe, Playa del Carmen

The ultimate in *cabaña* luxury: palm-roofed beach lodges with traditional Mexican fittings and five-star comforts. The pent-houses, in particular, are totally fabulous. *C/ 38 Norte por 5th Av • Map Q4 • (984) 873 0611, 1 800 942 0579 • www.shangri-lacaribe.net • $$$$$*

### 2 Las Palapas, Playa del Carmen

A seductive beach village just north of Playa del Carmen. It combines the palapa idea (a palm-roofed hut-type building) with luxurious fittings. Each unit is different, and the suites are especially attractive. There's a pretty beach bar and pool, and many water sports are available. *Map Q4 • C/34, by the beach • (984) 873 0584 • www.laspalapas.com.mx • $$$$$*

### 3 Cabañas María del Mar, Isla Mujeres

A little island of mellow comfort just behind Isla's Playa Norte, with the most popular bar on the beach, Buho's, attached. There's a main building with rooms or *cabaña*-bungalows; some are on the small side, but they're all attractive. Health treatments and massages are a specialty. *Map S1 • Av Carlos Lazo 1 • (998) 877 0179 • www.cabanasdelmar.com • $$$$$*

### 4 Rancho Sak Ol, Puerto Morelos

Equipped with their trademark "hanging beds" – solid beds on ropes that swing. The cabins have a typical beachcomber look. The use of an open kitchen is included, and yoga is offered. *Map R3 • (998) 871 0182 • www.ranchosakol.com • $$$$*

### 5 Boca Paila Camps, Tulum

Built according to strict environmental require-ments, this rustic lodge is just inside the Sian Ka'an Biosphere Reserve. Each "room" is actually a sturdy tent, set on a wooden platform. Bath-rooms are shared, but everything else is deluxe. The sea views are beautiful. *Beach Road, km 10.8 • (984) 877 8573 • www.cesiak.org • $$$$*

### 6 Cabañas Paamul, Playa del Carmen

Spacious beach rooms amid a camp site; some are in a modern building, others in palm-roofed huts. There's an enjoy-able bar-restaurant *(see p94)*, and the uncrowded beach is exquisite. *Map Q4 • (984) 875 1051 • www.paamul.com • $$$$*

### 7 Genesis Retreat, Ek-Balam

A beautiful eco-lodge, Genesis is a lush garden set around a bio-filtered pool, with rooms tucked away in the greenery. Bird-watching trips and tours to meet the Mayan neighbors are offered. *Off the northeast corner of the town plaza • (985) 852 7980 • www.genesisretreat.com • $$$*

### 8 Papaya Playa, Tulum

This long-standing cabaña hotel offers everything from a basic sand-floor cabin with a shared bath to private villas big enough for a family. Strung out on a wide stretch of un-crowded beach, most rooms have views directly onto the Caribbean. *Beach road, km 1 • (984) 130 1145 • www.papayaplaya.com• $$$*

### 9 Cuzan Guest House, Punta Allen

A small place, where the cabins all have bathrooms. It's often booked up by fishing groups, so check ahead. Enjoy the catch of the day in its sand-floored restaurant. *Map G5 • (983) 834 0358 • www.flyfishmx.com • $$$$*

### 10 Eco-Paraíso Xixim, near Celestún

This remarkable "eco-retreat" stands between coconut groves and a remote beach north of Celestún and is best accessed by 4-wheel drive. The cabins have lovely beach terraces. Nature and archeological tours are a specialty. *Map A2 • (988) 916 2100, (988) 916 2060 • www.ecoparaiso.com • $$$$$*

*Cabañas are palm-roofed huts by the sea, sometimes luxurious, sometimes basic; they are cooled by roof fans*

Left **Hotel Básico** Right **Hacienda Uayamón**

**Price Categories**

| For a standard, double room per night (with breakfast if included), taxes and extra charges. | |
|---|---|
| **$** | under $20 |
| **$$** | $20–$45 |
| **$$$** | $45–$80 |
| **$$$$** | $80–$130 |
| **$$$$$** | over $130 |

# TOP 10 Haciendas and Hip Hotels

### 1 Maroma, Punta Maroma

The Riviera's most opulent retreat is frequented by celebrities attracted to its 80 hectares (200 acres) of lush jungle and vast stretch of private beach. Rooms are truly vast, and there's a superb pool and a refined restaurant. Honeymooners and beauty-therapy addicts are well catered for. *Map R4 • (998) 872 8200 • www.maroma.net • $$$$$*

### 2 Hotel Básico, Playa del Carmen

The pinnacle of Playa style, the rooms in Básico have plush beds and floor-to-ceiling windows. Design details are fun and functional, from pink neon wall lights to the in-room Polaroid camera. The rooftop pool offers great views, and the seafood restaurant is excellent. *Av 5, at Calle 10 • (984) 879 4448 • www.hotelbasico.com • $$$$$*

### 3 Acanto Hotel & Suites, Playa del Carmen

Those looking for quality, privacy, and style can enjoy an exotic and environmentally friendly stay at this luxurious hotel. Each villa is resplendent in artistic decor, and fastidious attention is paid to the minutest detail. *Map Q4 • C/16, between Av 1 and Av 5 • (984) 873 1252 • www.acantohotels.com• $$$$$*

### 4 Hacienda San Antonio Chalanté, near Izamal

The Yucatán's restored hacienda-hotels are mostly in the luxury bracket, but this charming estate gives you the chance to sample local country life for much less. *Map D2 • (999) 132 7411 • www.haciendachalante.com • $$$*

### 5 Hacienda San José Cholul, near Mérida

A 17th-century estate 30 km (18 miles) east of Mérida, one of several aristocratic haciendas that have been converted by the Plan Group. Rooms are spacious, with Colonial-style furniture. *Map C2 • (999) 923 8089 • www.grupoplan.com • $$$$$*

### 6 Hacienda Puerta Campeche, Campeche

A selection of 17th-century houses have been restored to become the most original hotel in the area. Rooms and suites have satellite TV, and the accommodation boasts a restaurant, lounge bar, and pool. *Map A5 • C/59, No.71 • (999) 923 8089 • www.grupoplan.com • $$$$$*

### 7 Hacienda Xcanatún, near Mérida

This 18th-century hacienda offers 18 suites, each with a terrace and Jacuzzi, set in luxuriant gardens. There's a terrace bar, two pools, a spa, and a fabulous restaurant, the Casa de Piedra *(see pp70–71)*. *Map C2 • Xcanatún, 12 km north of Mérida • (999) 941 0213 • www.xcanatun.com • $$$$$*

### 8 Hacienda Temozón, near Uxmal

The most luxurious place to stay near Uxmal is provided by this Plan Group hacienda, 45 km (27 miles) north of the ruins. The 17th-century main house, terrace restaurant, and pool are spectacular. *Map C4 • (999) 923 8089 • www.grupoplan.com • $$$$$*

### 9 Hacienda Santa Rosa, near Mérida

In an area unknown to most visitors just west of the Mérida–Campeche road is another Plan hacienda, with 11 rooms and suites. The lofty, Colonial-style rooms are lovely, some with their own gardens. The restaurant, bars (in an old chapel), and pool are to match. *Map C2 • (999) 923 8089 • www.grupoplan.com • $$$$$*

### 10 Hacienda Uayamón, Campeche

The most isolated of the Plan haciendas, on an old *henequen* plantation (for ropemaking). The conversion has been done with style, and the pool – in a ruined, roofless building – is astonishing. *Map A5 • (999) 923 8089 • www.grupoplan.com • $$$$$*

***Note:** Unless otherwise stated, all hotels accept credit cards, have en-suite bathrooms, and air conditioning*

Left **Presidente Intercontinental** Center **Casa de los Sueños** Right **Hacienda Chichén**

# Top 10 Luxury Hotels

### 1 Ritz Carlton, Cancún

Top of the scale for sheer luxury in Cancún, the Ritz Carlton looks like the biggest Italian Renaissance palace ever built. All 365 rooms have ocean views, balconies, or terraces, and there's a private beach and five restaurants. *Map L5 • Blvd Kukulcán, km 14 • (998) 881 0808 • www.ritzcarlton.com • $$$$$*

### 2 JW Marriott, Cancún

The newest big hotel in Cancún is next door to the same company's slightly older Casa Magna. Expect state-of-the-art facilities, from the lavish health spa to the multitude of electronic accessories in the rooms. *Map K/L5 • Blvd Kukulcán, km 14.5 • (998) 848 9600 U.S. & Canada 1 800 228 9290 • www.marriotthotels.com • $$$$$*

### 3 Fiesta Americana Grand Coral Beach, Cancún

With cascades of greenery from its many balconies, the awesomely huge Coral Beach has 602 rooms and a thick catalogue of facilities, including tennis courts and its own jogging track. *Map L4 • Blvd Kukulcán, km 9.5 • (998) 881 3200 • www.fiestaamericana.com • $$$$$*

### 4 Hotel Secreto, Isla Mujeres

This small hotel is hidden away on the far side of Isla Mujeres. Though just a few minutes' walk from the center of town, the hotel is utterly quiet. Furnished with four-poster beds, the nine suites overlook the Caribbean. The hotel also has a long pool and outdoor "living room" bar. *Playa Norte • (998) 877 1039 • www.hotelsecreto.com • $$$$$*

### 5 Villa Rolandi, Isla Mujeres

Modest-sized hotel on the western side of Isla's Laguna Macax, with its own beach and boat landing stage, and superb views across to Cancún. No children under 13 are admitted – honeymoons are a specialty. Each balcony has a Jacuzzi. *Map L1/2 • Fraccionamiento Laguna Mar • (998) 877 0700 • www.villarolandi.com • $$$$$*

### 6 Casa de los Sueños, Isla Mujeres

A secluded lodge toward the southern end of Isla Mujeres. Its eight spacious rooms, pool, and oceanside terrace are of contemporary Mexican style: stunning to look at and supremely comfortable. *Map L2 • Carretera Garrafón • (998) 877 0651 or (01800) 505 0252 • www.casadelossuenosresort.com • $$$$$*

### 7 Presidente Intercontinental, Cozumel

Big for Cozumel but smallish by Cancún standards (253 rooms), this is one of the island's longest-established hotels. It enjoys a superb location with its own beach and marina. Diving, snorkeling, and fishing trips can be arranged. *Map R5 • Carretera a Chankanaab, km 6.5 • (987) 872 9500 • www.intercontinental.com • $$$$$*

### 8 Hacienda Chichén, Chichén Itzá

Set in an old colonial hacienda next to the ruins of Chichén Itzá. Most of the airy rooms are in bungalows used by archeologists in the 1920s and have a faded charm. *Map E3 • (985) 851 0046 • www.haciendachichen.com • $$$$$*

### 9 Fiesta Americana, Mérida

Mérida's premiere hotel is modern but built in an ornate French-mansion style, with a spectacular stained-glass atrium. Rooms are spacious and well-equipped. *Map C2 • Paseo de Montejo 451 • (999) 942 1111 • www.fiestamericana.com • $$$$$*

### 10 Hacienda Uxmal

This big hotel near the Uxmal ruins was built in the 1950s and has a gracious style extending through airy, colonial-style patios. The spacious, cool rooms have characterful wooden furniture and verandas, and the service is very charming. *Map C4 • (998) 887 2450 • www.mayaland.com • $$$$$*

**Note:** *Nearly all the luxury hotels in Cancún offer heavily discounted short-break packages through agents abroad, especially in the U.S.*

Reef Resort

**Price Categories**

For a standard, double room per night (with breakfast if included), taxes and extra charges.

| | |
|---|---|
| $ | under US$20 |
| $$ | US$20–$45 |
| $$$ | US$45–$80 |
| $$$$ | US$80–$130 |
| $$$$$ | over US$130 |

# TOP 10 Resort Hotels

### 1 Gran Oasis, Cancún

With 1,316 rooms, everything about this hotel-resort is on a grand scale. Three giant pyramids make up the main buildings; there are eight restaurants, 13 bars, the Up & Down nightclub, and the pool is one of the biggest in Latin America. A big range of watersports and theme parties complete the picture. *Map K5 • Blvd Kukulcán, km 15.5 • (998) 885 0867 • www.oasishoteles.com • $$$$$*

### 2 Club Med Cancún

Opened in the early days of Cancún, this spacious site has the typical Club-Med range of sports facilities – enough even when the 456 rooms fill up – and youth-oriented entertainment including a techno disco. *Map K6 • Punta Nizuc, Blvd Kukulcán, km 20 • (998) 881 8200 • www.clubmed.com • $$$$$*

### 3 Moon Palace Golf and Resort, near Cancún

The biggest all-inclusive resort of all, with 2,131 beach-house-style rooms. It offers every possible activity and 14 restaurants – all crowded. *Map R3 • (998) 881 6000 • www.palaceresorts.com* • $$$$$

### 4 Marina and Spa El Cid Riviera Maya, Puerto Morelos

Located right on the ocean, this new hotel combines colonial and modern architecture. Guests can go snorkeling at the Puerto Morelos National Reef Park in front of the hotel. *Blvd El Cid Unidad 15, Puerto Morelos • (998) 872 8999 • www.elcid.com • $$$$$*

### 5 Reef Resort, Playacar

A good deal cheaper than most places offering an all-meals-included plan. Rooms and food are relatively basic, but it has a great beach location and a fine pool. Its low prices and simple style have won it many fans. *Map H3 & Q4 • (984) 873 4120 • www.thereefresorts.com • $$$$$*

### 6 Royal Hideaway, Playa del Carmen

This all-inclusive resort prides itself on its food, with a choice of gourmet Spanish, Asian, and Italian restaurants. The rooms come with ceiling fans, wicker furniture, and wood porches. *Lote 6, Playacar • (984) 873 4500 • www.royalhideaway.com • $$$$$*

### 7 Iberostar Cozumel

The 300-room Iberostar, opened in 1999, is well located for snorkeling and diving in the southwest corner of the island, near Punta Francesa, and faces an especially fine beach. Like the Tucán, it offers a big range of activities. *Map R6 • (987) 872 9900 • www.iberostarcaribe.com • $$$$$*

### 8 Barceló Maya Beach Resort, Puerto Aventuras

Another giant, split into two: the Barceló Maya Beach (612 rooms) and the Barceló Maya Garden next door (408 rooms). They share over 2 km (1.5 miles) of beach and offer a lot on-site for the all-inclusive rates. Highlights include a nightclub under a giant palapa plant and a luxurious beachside buffet. *Map Q5 • (984) 875 1500 • www.barcelo.com • $$$$$*

### 9 Secrets Capri Riviera Cancun, Playa del Carmen

Only a few minutes north of Playa del Carmen, this adults-only, all-inclusive resort still feels secluded. The hotel has excellent à la carte restaurants and a beautiful beach. *Carretera Federal 370, km 299 • (998) 873 4880 • www.secretsresorts.com/capri • $$$$$*

### 10 Akumal Beach Resort, Akumal

Medium-sized resort with an exquisite, large pool that snakes beside some of the rooms. It's only a short walk from Akumal village along the beach, so those who appreciate the convenience of all-inclusives can also wander out whenever they wish. *Map P5 • (984) 875 7500 • www.akumalbeachresort.com • $$$$$*

***Note:** All resort hotels listed here have all-inclusive rates, covering some or all meals, drinks, and activities such as snorkeling and diving*

Left **Caribe Internacional** Center **Hotel Flamingo** Right **Piedra Escondida**

# Top 10 Mid-Range Hotels on the Riviera

## 1 Plaza Caribe, Cancún

This big hotel's main selling point is that it's right opposite the bus station in Ciudad Cancún and so is always popular. Despite being in such a traffic-heavy area, it's surprisingly peaceful inside, with pretty gardens, a nice pool, and attractively furnished rooms. *Map J3 • Av Tulum No.19, corner of Av Uxmal • (998) 884 1377 • www.hotelplaza caribe.com • $$$$*

## 2 Caribe Internacional, Cancún

This 80-room hotel is in one of the liveliest parts of Ciudad Cancún, near the market and next to Av Yaxchilán's "restaurant row." Rooms are modern, simple, spacious, and bright, and there's a good pool, making this great value in sometimes over-priced Cancún. *Map J3 • Av Yaxchilán 36–7 • (998) 884 3999 • www.caribe internacional.com • $$$*

## 3 Villa Kiin, Isla Mujeres

All the rooms are different – some are on the beach, some are like separate little beach-houses – but all are comfortable and fitted with Mexican textiles. It's in a delightful location, facing the placid Playa Secreto lagoon, and there's snorkel gear for guests' use. *Map L1 • C/Zazil-Ha No.129, Playa Norte • (998) 877 0045 • www.villakiin. com.mx • $$$$$*

## 4 Hotel Faro Viejo, Holbox

Holbox's best hotel is two blocks away from the main street. The Mexican-style rooms are a real pleasure: doubles and twins upstairs have balconies, suites below have terraces and kitchenettes. The French-Mexican owners are very welcoming, and there's a great restaurant. *Map G1 • C/Juárez, on the beach • (984) 875 2217 • www.faro viejoholbox.com.mx • $$$$*

## 5 Hotel Flamingo, Cozumel

Began as a dive hotel and offers a range of packages for divers. Even if you're not a scuba nut, it's a comfortable place, with well-cared-for rooms and a bar and rooftop terrace-lounge. *Map R5 • San Miguel de Cozumel • (987) 872 1264 • www. hotelflamingo.com • $$$$*

## 6 Casa Tucán, Playa del Carmen

Seems small from the street, but inside is a maze of patios, gardens, and spiral staircases, leading to a leaf-shaded pool. Rooms are cosy and colorful. The friendly German owners offer packages with the Yucatek Divers school *(see p124)*. *Map Q4 • C/4, between Av 10 and Av 15 • (984) 873 0283 • www.casatucan.de • $$$*

## 7 Mom's Hotel, Playa del Carmen

Texan Ricco Merkle's long-running hotel is a friendly home from home. The rooms have been going a few years but are comfortable and pretty, and there's a tiny pool and a rooftop bar that's a great place for meeting people. *Map Q4 • Av 30, by C/4 • (984) 873 0315 • www.momshotel.com • $$$*

## 8 Aquatech – Villas de Rosa, Akumal

Owners Nancy and Tony de Rosa are the foremost cave-diving specialists on the Riviera, and many of their guests dive. The place is also well equipped for families. *Map P5 • Km 115, Carrt. Puerto Aventuras–Akuma • (984) 875 9020 • www.cenotes. com • $$$$*

## 9 Tankah Dive Inn

This laid-back hotel on the Riviera has only a few rooms, but they're all comfortable and full of character. Diving is a big attraction, of course, but it's ok just to sit on the beach and sample the fine cuisine. *Map P6 • Bahía Tankah No.16, Tulum • (984) 100 0703 • www. tankah.com • $$$$$*

## 10 Piedra Escondida, Tulum

Nine rooms, in two-story *cabaña*-style beach huts, all with good showers and entrancing views. The restaurant serves a mix of Italian and Mexican food. *Map P6 • Km 3.5 Tulum Ruinas, Boca Paila Rd • (984) 130 9932 • www.piedra escondida.com • $$$$$*

**Note**: *Unless otherwise stated, all hotels accept credit cards, have en-suite bathrooms, and air conditioning*

Ecotel Quinta Regia

**Price Categories**

| For a standard, double room per night (with breakfast if included), taxes, and extra charges. | |
|---|---|
| $ | under US$20 |
| $$ | US$20–$45 |
| $$$ | US$45–$80 |
| $$$$ | US$80–$130 |
| $$$$$ | over US$130 |

# Top 10 Mid-Range Hotels Elsewhere

## 1 Ecotel Quinta Regia, Valladolid

Built in a Neo-Colonial style, this hotel combines a colorful Mexican look with modern facilities. Lush gardens are overlooked by the best rooms. The pool is secluded, and the restaurant makes use of garden produce *(see p103)*. *Map E3 • C/40 No. 160A, between C/27 and C/29 • (985) 856 3476 • www.ecotelquintaregia.com.mx • $$$*

## 2 El Mesón del Marqués, Valladolid

Valladolid's classic hotel occupies one of its finest old colonial houses, with rooms set around several flower-filled, elegant patios. There's a great restaurant *(see p103)* and a pool. *Map E3 • C/39 No. 203, on Parque Principal • (985) 856 2073 • www.elmesondelmarques.com • $$$*

## 3 Hotel Dolores Alba, Chichén Itzá

The best-value place to stay near Chichén, this roadside hotel has bright rooms, a restaurant, and two pools. The owners also run a hotel in Mérida *(entry 7)*, through which bookings can be made. *Map E3 • Hwy 180, 3 km east of Chichén Itzá • (985) 858 1555 • www.doloresalba.com • $$$*

## 4 Hotel San Felipe, San Felipe

Staying near Río Lagartos used to be a problem, so this hotel is a welcome arrival. The water-side restaurant is a great place to lounge, and all the spacious rooms have a sitting area. *Map E1 • C/9, between C/14 and C/16 • (986) 862 2027 • $$*

## 5 La Misión de Fray Diego, Mérida

This grand 17th-century house has been expensively converted with a mix of antiques and all-modern bathrooms, a pool and other services. Some rooms have a real Spanish-mansion air; others are less exciting, and prices vary accordingly. *Map C2 • C/61 No. 524, between C/64 and C/66 • (999) 924 1111 or (01800) 866 392935(from the U.S. and Canada) • www.lamisiondefraydiego.com • $$$$*

## 6 Hotel Marionetas, Mérida

Once a puppet theatre, the colonial building that forms the core of this hotel has been beautifully restored with rooms painted in pastel shades. The hotel has a large pool and serves delicious breakfasts. *C/49 No.516, between C/62 & C/64 • (999) 928 3377 • www.hotelmarionetas.com • $$$$*

## 7 Hotel Dolores Alba, Mérida

One of Mérida's most popular hotels, with a relaxed atmosphere. Beyond an elderly façade, the renovated rooms set around the pool are surprisingly modern and a great bargain. *Map C2 • C/63 No. 464, between C/52 and C/54 • (999) 928 5650 • www.doloresalba.com • $$$*

## 8 Casa Hamaca, Valladolid

This large guesthouse with its garden of trees has a countryside feel. It offers not just comfortable beds, but also full spa services and healthy breakfasts. *Parque San Juan, C/49 No. 202-A at C/40 • (985) 856 5287 • www.casahamaca.com • $$$*

## 9 Club Med-Villas Arqueológicas, Uxmal

The Villas Arqueológicas are a small chain of hotels at some of the ancient Mayan sites, all built in old-Mexican, hacienda style, with charming rooms and exuberant gardens. The Uxmal branch is exceptional value. *Map C4 • (997) 976 2040 • www.clubmed.com • $$$$*

## 10 Hotel Baluartes, Campeche

Campeche has a limited selection of hotels. This lofty 1970s building on the seafront is more comfortable than most. Be sure to get a room with sea view, to catch the superb sunsets over the Gulf of Mexico. *Map A5 • Av 16 de Septiembre 128 • (981) 816 3911 • www.baluartes.com.mx • $$$$*

**Note:** *Though breakfast is not generally included in room prices, it is becoming a more common feature of Yucatán hotels*

Left **Tamarindo** Center **Casa San Juan** Right **Casa Mexilio**

# Top 10 Guesthouses and B&Bs

### 1 Amigo's B&B, Cozumel

Three *cabaña*-style rooms, all with kitchenettes, fridges, and terraces, set around a pool and lovely garden. It's especially suited to families: breakfasts (included) are served in a garden palapa (palm-roofed gazebo). *Map R5 • C/7 sur No.571A, San Miguel de Cozumel • (987) 872 3868 • www.bacalar.net • $$$$*

### 2 Tamarindo, Cozumel

A lot of energy and style have been put into the house and its sheltered garden by its Mexican-French owners. Each of the five pretty rooms has its own character, there's an open kitchen and ample breakfasts, and they have many happy clients. They also run Palapas Amaranto nearby, with self-contained suites. *Map R5 • Rojo Gomez and Lázaro Cárdenas • (987) 872 3614 • $$$*

### 3 Amar Inn, Puerto Morelos

This sea-front bed & breakfast has lovely views and offers a rustic atmosphere. The decor is traditional and each room is painted a different color. Arrangements can be made for tours to nearby tourist spots. The right place for those looking for something typical of the region. *Map R3 • Av Rojo Gómez • (998) 871 0026 • $$$*

### 4 Flycatcher Inn, Santa Elena

This pretty bed & breakfast is decorated with locally made furniture and wall hangings. The owners are very knowledgeable about the nearby archaeological sites. *Calle 20, off Hwy-261 • (997) 102 0865 • www.flycatcherinn.com • $$*

### 5 Posada Sirena, Punta Allen

Punta Allen is about the most beachcomberish destination imaginable, and this guest house hits the appropriate note, with a stay-as-long-as-you-want feel from owner Serena, a real character. Her two cabins have kitchens and the essential hammocks. She can arrange fishing and diving. *Map G5 • Fax (984) 877 8521 • www.casasirena.com • $$*

### 6 Macanché, Izamal

Izamal is a tranquil town in any case, but the walled garden that contains this B&B, is especially soothing. Little bungalows are dotted about the garden, each imaginatively decorated; one has a kitchen. *Map D2 • C/22 No. 305, between C/33 & C/35 • (988) 954 0287 • www.macanche.com • $$$*

### 7 Casa Mexilio, Mérida

This is a special guesthouse in a fine old building. The hallways and eight rooms are full of traditional furniture and antiques, and the Mexican-American owners have added original touches, including a cave-like pool and two bars, one on the roof. *Map C2 • C/68 No. 495, between C/59 & C/57 • (999) 928 2505 • www.casamexilio.com • $$$*

### 8 Casa San Juan, Mérida

Once the home of an old Mérida family, this 19th-century house has been beautifully restored with seven charming, lofty-ceilinged rooms. *Map C2 • C/62 No. 545, between C/69 & C/71 • (999) 923 6823 • www.casasanjuan.com • No air con in some rooms • $$$*

### 9 Luz en Yucatán, Mérida

Once part of a convent, this house is now an urban retreat with modern apartments and small pool, at bargain prices. Health therapies can be arranged. *Map C2 • C/55 No. 499, between C/58 & C/60 • (999) 924 0035 • www.luzenyucatán.com • $$$*

### 10 Medio Mundo, Mérida

Located in the heart of town, this colonial house is uniquely decorated. The ten rooms are simply furnished and face the central patio. Every room is en suite. *Map C2 • C/55 No.533 • (999) 924 5472 • www.hotelmediomundo.com • No air con in some rooms • $$$$*

***Note:** Unless otherwise stated, all hotels accept credit cards, have en-suite bathrooms, and air conditioning*

**Price Categories**

| For a standard, double room per night (with breakfast if included), taxes, and extra charges. | | |
|---|---|---|
| | $ | under US-$20 |
| | $$ | US$20-$45 |
| | $$$ | US$45-$80 |
| | $$$$ | US$80-$130 |
| | $$$$$ | over US-$130 |

Left **Posada Amor** Right **Cabañas Copal**

# Top 10 Budget Accommodation

### 1 The Weary Traveler, Cancún

Open since 2000, this is affiliated to the Mexican hostel association AMAJ. It has 64 dorm-style beds. Bright and clean, good shared showers, and an open kitchen. *Map J3 • C/Palmeras 30, off Av Uxmal • (998) 887 0191 • www.mexicohostels.com.mx • $$*

### 2 Hotel Carmelina, Isla Mujeres

The laid-back Carmelina has been welcoming budget travelers for years. Arranged around a big patio, rooms are simple but cheerful. All have showers, and some even air con. *Map L1 • Isla Town, between Av Abasolo and Av Madero • (998) 877 0006 • No air con in some rooms • $$*

### 3 Hotel Pepita, Cozumel

Friendly and helpful owners make the difference in this big, popular hotel. Rooms are well cared for and have such extras as air con and small fridges, and complimentary coffee is provided. *Map R5 • San Miguel de Cozumel • (987) 872 0098 • $$*

### 4 Posada Amor, Puerto Morelos

Featuring Puerto Morelos' best low-priced rooms, Posada Amor has a friendly feel and popular restaurant. The rooms come in different shapes and sizes. *Map R3 • On the plaza • (998) 871 0033 • No air con in some rooms • www.geocities/posadaamor • $$$*

### 5 Cabañas La Ruina, Playa del Carmen

A remarkable survivor from Playa's hippy days, gripping on to its great beach location in the face of glossier developments. Inside two garden enclosures you have a choice between simple *cabañas*, with or without showers, or hammock space under a big, mixed-sex palapa. *Map Q4 • C/2, between Av 5 & the beach • No air con or en-suite • (984) 873 0405 • $$$*

### 6 Cabañas Copal, Tulum

A well-run *cabaña* cluster with 32 cabins around a palm grove by the beach. A choice of dorms, double, or singles (with or without showers), and family-sized huts. Some have a sea view. It has a restaurant and two bars, and a relaxed feel. *Map P6 • Beach Rd, km 3.5 • (984) 871 2750 • www.cabanascopal.com • $$$*

### 7 Albergue La Candelaria, Valladolid

Affiliated to AMAJ, this newish hostel in a pretty, old house has excellent, bright dorm rooms, good shared bathrooms, a lounge and patio area, free coffee, and cheap Internet access. *Map E3 • C/35 No.201F, between C/42 and C/44 • (985) 856 2267 • www.hostels.com.mx • $*

### 8 Nómadas Hostel, Mérida

Challenging the cheap hotels of Mérida for value, this hostel has bright, airy dorm rooms and a few doubles. There's also an open kitchen, a lounge space, and cheap Internet access. *Map C2 • C/62 No. 433, by C/51 • (999) 924 5223 • www.hostels.com • $$*

### 9 Hotel Plaza, Ticul

Pleasantly easygoing hotel on Ticul's main square. Rooms are spacious and comfortable, with good bathrooms, fans or air con, and TVs; get one overlooking the square. *Map C4 • C/23 No.202, by the plaza • (997) 972 0484 • www.hotelplazayucatan.com • $$*

### 10 Bungalows Sacbé, near Uxmal

The best budget accommodation really near to Uxmal is provided at this very welcoming site just south of the village of Santa Elena. The Mexican-French couple who live here offer camping space (with good showers and solar power), dorm beds, and very pretty doubles, with showers, in cabins. Meals, equally a bargain, are also available. *Map C4 • near Santa Elena • (985) 858 1281 • $$*

**Note:** *Most hostels require payment in cash*

# General Index

Page numbers in **bold** type refer to main entries.

**D**

# Acknowledgements

**The Author**
Nick Rider is a freelance travel writer and editor, based in London.

Produced by
BLUE ISLAND PUBLISHING,
London
www.blueisland.co.uk

**Editorial Director**
Rosalyn Thiro
**Art Director**
Stephen Bere
**Associate Editors**
Michael Ellis, Jane Simmonds
**Designers**
Lee Redmond, Ian Midson
**Picture Research**
Ellen Root
**Research Assistance**
Amaia Allende
**Proofreader**
Stephanie Driver
**Fact-checker**
Andrea Traconis
**Indexer**
Charlotte Rundall

**Main Photographer**
Demetrio Carrasco
**Additional Photography**
Eva Gleason, Miguel Nuñez, José Eduardo Cervantes Pérez, Clive Streeter, Linda Whitwam and Michael Zebe
**Cartography**
Martin Darlison and Tom Coulson at Encompass Graphics

AT DORLING KINDERSLEY
**Publisher**
Douglas Amrine
**Publishing Managers**
Fay Franklin, Kate Poole
**Senior Art Editor**
Marisa Renzullo
**Cartographic Editor**
Casper Morris
**DTP**
Jason Little
**Production**
Melanie Dowland

**Design and Editorial Assistance**
Nicola Erdpresser, Eva Gleason, Katharina Hahn, Victoria Heyworth-Dunne, Sands Publishing Solutions, Quadrum Solutions (pvt) Ltd, Rada Radojicic, Sadie Smith, Leah Tether, Conrad van Dyk, Karen Villabona

**Picture Credits**
Dorling Kindersley would like to thank all the many establishments covered in this book for their assistance and kind permission for the producers to take photographs in their establishments.

Placement Key: t=top; tl=top left; tr=top right; tc=top center; tcl=top center left; c=center; cr=center right; b=bottom; bl=bottom left; br=bottom right.

PABLO DE AGUINACO: 63c, 64tr; ALAMY IMAGES: Johan Furusjö 82tr; Gordon Sinclair 110tl; ECOTEL QUINTA REGIA: 103tc; GENESIS ECO-OASIS: 126tr; EVA MARIA GLEASON: 70d, 118tcr, 119c, 132c; ANDREAS GROSS: 65bl; HOTEL BASICO: Undine Pröhl 127tl; JUSTIN KERR: 25ca; ENRICO MARTINO: 29b; JOSE LUIS MORENO: 47tl, 47br; MEXICANA AIRLINES: 115tl; MINDEN PICTURES: Claus Meyer 7tl, 21b; GRUPO LA PARRILLA: 70c, 82tc; LA SANTANERA: 61t, 81tr; NANCY SEFTON: 46b, 47tr; SEXTO SOL: Alberto Rios Szalay: 64c; HENN STERLIN: 36tl; MIREILLE VAUTIER: 6t, 25cb, 30tc, 36tr, 36b.

# Phrase Book

## In an Emergency

| | | |
|---|---|---|
| Help! | **¡Socorro!** | soh-**koh**-roh |
| Stop! | **¡Pare!** | **pah**-reh |
| Call a doctor! | **¡Llame a un médico!** | **yah**-meh ah **oon meh**-dee-koh |
| Call an ambulance! | **¡Llame una ambulancia!** | **yah**-meh ah **oonah** ahm-boo-**lahn**-see-ah |
| Call the fire department! | **¡Llame a los bomberos!** | **yah**-meh ah lohs bohm-**beh**-rohs |
| policeman | **el policía** | ehl poh-lee-**see**-ah |

## Communication Essentials

| | | |
|---|---|---|
| Yes | **Sí** | see |
| No | **No** | noh |
| Please | **Por favor** | pohr fah-**vohr** |
| Thank you | **Gracias** | **grah**-see-ahs |
| Excuse me | **Perdone** | pehr-**doh**-neh |
| Hello | **Hola** | **oh**-lah |
| Bye (casual) | **Chau** | chau |
| Goodbye | **Adiós** | ah-dee-**ohs** |
| What? | **¿Qué?** | **keh** |
| When? | **¿Cuándo?** | **kwahn**-doh |
| Why? | **¿Por qué?** | pohr-**keh** |
| Where? | **¿Dónde?** | **dohn**-deh |
| How are you? | **¿Cómo está usted?** | **koh**-moh ehs-**tah** oos-**tehd** |
| Very well, thank you | **Muy bien, gracias** | mwee bee-**ehn grah**-see-ahs |
| Pleased to meet you | **Mucho gusto** | **moo**-choh **goo**-stoh |
| See you soon | **Hasta pronto** | ahs-tah **prohn**-toh |
| I'm sorry | **Lo siento** | loh see-**ehn**-toh |

## Useful Phrases

| | | |
|---|---|---|
| That's fine | **Está bien** | ehs-**tah** bee-**ehn** |
| Great/fantastic! | **¡Qué bien!** | **keh** bee-**ehn** |
| Where is/are…? | **¿Dónde está/están…?** | **dohn**-deh ehs-**tah**/ehs-**tahn** |
| How far is it to…? | **¿Cuántos metros/kilómetros hay de aquí a…?** | **kwahn**-tohs **meh**-trohs/kee-**loh**-meh-trohs **eye** deh ah-**kee** ah |
| Which way is it to…? | **¿Por dónde se va a…?** | pohr **dohn**-deh seh **vah** ah |
| Do you speak English? | **¿Habla inglés?** | **ah**-blah een-**glehs** |
| I don't understand | **No comprendo/entiendo** | noh kohm-**prehn**-doh |
| I would like | **Quisiera/Me gustaría** | kee-see-**yehr**-ah meh goo-stah-**ree** ah |

## Useful Words

| | | |
|---|---|---|
| big | **grande** | **grahn**-deh |
| small | **pequeño/a** | peh-**keh**-nyoh/nyah |
| hot | **caliente** | kah-lee-**ehn**-teh |
| cold | **frío/a** | **free**-oh/ah |
| good | **bueno/a** | **bweh**-noh/nah |
| bad | **malo/a** | **mah**-loh/lah |
| open | **abierto/a** | ah-bee-**ehr**-toh/tah |
| closed | **cerrado/a** | sehr-**rah**-doh/dah |
| full | **lleno/a** | **yeh**-noh/nah |
| empty | **vacío/a** | **vah**-see-oh/ah |
| left | **izquierda** | ees-key-**ehr**-dah |
| right | **derecha** | deh-**reh**-chah |
| (keep) straight ahead | **(siga) derecho** | (**see**-gah) deh-**reh**-choh |
| near | **cerca** | **sehr**-kah |
| far | **lejos** | **leh**-hohs |
| more | **más** | **mahs** |
| less | **menos** | **meh**-nohs |
| entrance | **entrada** | ehn-**trah**-dah |
| exit | **salida** | sah-**lee**-dah |
| elevator | **el ascensor** | **ehl** ah-sehn-**sohr** |
| toilets | **baños/** | bah-nyohs/ |
| women's | **de damas** | deh **dah**-mahs |
| men's | **de caballeros** | deh kah-bah-**yeh**-rohs |

## Post Offices and Banks

| | | |
|---|---|---|
| Where can I change money? | **¿Dónde puedo cambiar dinero?** | **dohn**-deh **pweh**-doh kahm-bee-**ahr** dee-**neh**-roh |
| How much is the postage to…? | **¿Cuánto cuesta enviar una carta a…?** | **kwahn**-toh **kweh**-stah ehn-vee-**yahr oo**-nah **kahr**-tah ah |
| I need stamps | **Necesito estampillas** | neh-seh-**see**-toh ehs-tahm-**pee**-yahs |

## Shopping

| | | |
|---|---|---|
| How much does this cost? | **¿Cuánto cuesta esto?** | **kwahn**-toh **kwehs**-tah **ehs**-toh |
| I would like… | **Me gustaría…** | meh goos-tah-**ree**-ah |
| Do you have? | **¿Tienen?** | tee-**yeh**-nehn |
| Do you take credit cards/traveler's checks? | **¿Aceptan tarjetas de crédito/cheques de viajero?** | ahk-**sehp**-tahn tahr-**heh**-tahs deh **kreh**-dee-toh/**cheh**-kehs deh vee-ah-**heh**-roh |
| I am looking for… | **Estoy buscando…** | **ehs**-tohy boos-**kahn**-doh |
| expensive | **caro** | **kahr**-oh |
| cheap | **barato** | bah-**rah**-toh |
| white | **blanco** | **blahn**-koh |
| black | **negro** | **neh**-groh |
| red | **rojo** | **roh**-hoh |
| yellow | **amarillo** | ah-mah-**ree**-yoh |
| green | **verde** | **vehr**-deh |
| blue | **azul** | ah-**sool** |

| | | |
|---|---|---|
| antique store | **la tienda de antigüedades** | lah tee-**ehn**-dah deh ahn-tee-gweh-**dah**-dehs |
| bakery | **la panadería** | lah pah-nah-deh **ree**-ah |
| bank | **el banco** | ehl **bahn**-koh |
| bookstore | **la librería** | lah lee-breh-**ree**-ah |
| butcher's | **la carnicería** | lah kahr-nee-seh-**ree**-ah |
| cake store | **la pastelería** | lah pahs-teh-leh-**ree**-ah |
| jeweler's | **la joyería** | lah hoh-yeh-**ree**-yah |
| market | **el tianguis/ mercado** | ehl tee-ahn-goo-ees/mehr-**kah**-doh |
| newsstand | **el kiosko de prensa** | ehl kee-**ohs**-koh deh **prehn**-sah |
| post office | **la oficina de correos** | lah oh-fee-**see**-nah deh kohr-**reh**-ohs |
| shoe store | **la zapatería** | lah sah-pah-teh-**ree**-ah |
| supermarket | **el supermercado** | ehl soo-pehr-mehr-**kah**-doh |
| travel agency | **la agencia de viajes** | lah ah-**hehn**-see-ah deh vee-**ah**-hehs |

## Transportation

| | | |
|---|---|---|
| When does the… leave? | **¿A qué hora sale el…?** | ah **keh oh**-rah **sah**-leh ehl |
| Where is bus stop? | **¿Dónde está la parada de buses?** | **dohn**-deh ehs-the **tah** lah pah-**rah**-dah deh **boo**-sehs |
| Is there a bus /train to…? | **¿Hay un camión/ tren a...?** | **eye oon** kah-mee-**ohn/trehn** ah |
| platform | **el andén** | ehl ahn-**dehn** |
| ticket office | **la taquilla** | lah tah-**kee**-yah |
| round-trip ticket | **un boleto de ida y vuelta** | **oon** boh-**leh**-toh deh **ee**-dah ee voo-**ehl**-tah |
| one-way ticket | **un boleto de ida solamente** | **oon** boh-**leh**-toh deh **ee**-dah soh-lah-**mehn**-teh |
| airport | **el aeropuerto** | ehl ah-ehr-oh-poo- |

## Sightseeing

| | | |
|---|---|---|
| art gallery | **el museo de arte** | ehl moo-**seh**-oh deh **ahr**-teh |
| beach | **la playa** | lah **plah**-yah |
| cathedral | **la catedral** | lah kah-teh-**drahl** |
| church | **la iglesia/ la basílica** | lah ee-**gleh**-see-ah/ lah bah-**see**-lee-kah |
| garden | **el jardín** | ehl hahr-**deen** |
| museum | **el museo** | ehl moo-**seh**-oh |
| pyramid | **la pirámide** | lah pee-**rah**-meed |
| ruins | **las ruinas** | lahs roo-**ee**-nahs |

| | | |
|---|---|---|
| tourist information office | **la oficina de turismo** | lah oh-fee-**see**-nah deh too-**rees**-moh |
| ticket | **la entrada** | lah ehn-**trah**-dah |
| guide (person) | **el/la guía** | ehl/lah **gee**-ah |
| guide (book) | **la guía** | lah **gee**-ah |
| map | **el mapa** | ehl **mah** -pah |
| taxi stand | **sitio de taxis** | **see**-tee-on deh **tahk**-sees |

## Staying in a Hotel

| | | |
|---|---|---|
| Do you have a vacant room? | **¿Tienen una habitación libre?** | tee-**eh**-nehn **oo**-nah ah-bee-tah-see-**ohn lee**-breh |
| double room | **habitación doble** | ah-bee-tah-see-**ohn doh**-bleh |
| single room | **habitación sencilla** | ah-bee-tah-see-**ohn** sehn-**see**-yah |
| room with a bath | **habitación con baño** | ah-bee-tah-see-**ohn** kohn **bah**-nyoh |
| shower | **la ducha** | lah **doo**-chah |
| I have a reservation | **Tengo una habitación reservada** | tehn-goh **oo**-nah ah-bee-tah-see-**ohn** reh-sehr-**vah**-dah |
| key | **la llave** | lah **yah**-veh |

## Eating Out

| | | |
|---|---|---|
| Have you got a table for… | **¿Tienen mesa para…?** | tee-**eh**-nehn meh-sah pah-**rah** |
| I want to reserve a table | **Quiero reservar una mesa** | kee-eh-roh reh-sehr-**vahr oo**-nah **meh**-sah |
| The bill, please | **La cuenta, por favor** | lah **kwehn**-tah pohr fah-**vohr** |
| I am a vegetarian | **Soy vegetariano/a** | soy veh-heh-tah-ree-**ah**-no/na |
| waiter/waitress | **mesero/a** | meh-**seh**-roh/rah |
| menu | **la carta** | lah **kahr**-tah |
| wine list | **la carta de vinos** | lah **kahr**-tah deh **vee**-nohs |
| glass | **un vaso** | **oon vah**-soh |
| bottle | **una botella** | **oo**-nah boh-**teh**-yah |
| knife | **un cuchillo** | **oon** koo-**chee**-yoh |
| fork | **un tenedor** | **oon** teh-neh-**dohr** |
| spoon | **una cuchara** | **oo**-nah koo-**chah**-rah |
| breakfast | **el desayuno** | ehl deh-sah-**yoo**-noh |
| lunch | **la comida** | lah koh-**mee**-dah |
| dinner | **la cena** | lah **seh**-nah |
| main course | **el plato fuerte** | ehl **plah**-toh foo-**ehr**-teh |
| starters | **las entradas** | lahs ehn-**trah**-das |
| dish of the day | **el plato del día** | ehl **plah**-toh dehl **dee**-ah |
| tip | **la propina** | lah proh-**pee**-nah |
| Is service included? | **¿El servicio está incluido?** | ehl sehr-**vee**-see-oh ehs-**tah** een-kloo-**ee**-doh |

*Bold letters in the pronunciation guides (right columns) indicate the stressed syllable.*

## Menu Decoder

| | | |
|---|---|---|
| **el aceite** | ah-**see-eh**-teh | oil |
| **las aceitunas** | ah-seh-**toon**-ahs | olives |
| **el agua mineral** | **ah**-gwa mee-neh-**rahl** | mineral water |
| **sin gas/con gas** | seen gas /kohn gas | still/sparkling |
| **el ajo** | **ah**-hoh | garlic |
| **el arroz** | ahr-**rohs** | rice |
| **el azúcar** | ah-**soo**-kahr | sugar |
| **el plátano** | **pla**-tah-noh | banana |
| **una bebida** | beh-**bee**-dah | drink |
| **el café** | kah-**feh** | coffee |
| **la carne** | **kahr**-neh | meat |
| **la cebolla** | seh-**boh**-yah | onion |
| **la cerveza** | sehr-**veh**-sah | beer |
| **el cerdo** | **sehr**-doh | pork |
| **el chocolate** | choh-koh-**lah**-teh | chocolate |
| **la ensalada** | ehn-sah-**lah**-dah | salad |
| **la fruta** | **froo**-tah | fruit |
| **el helado** | eh-**lah**-doh | ice cream |
| **el huevo** | oo-**eh**-voh | egg |
| **el jugo** | ehl **hoo**-goh | juice |
| **la langosta** | lahn-**gohs**-tah | lobster |
| **la leche** | **leh**-cheh | milk |
| **la mantequilla** | mahn-teh-**kee**-yah | butter |
| **la manzana** | mahn-**sah**-nah | apple |
| **los mariscos** | mah-**rees**-kohs | seafood |
| **la naranja** | nah-**rahn**-hah | orange |
| **el pan** | **pahn** | bread |
| **las papas** | **pah**-pahs | potatoes |
| **el pescado** | pehs-**kah**-doh | fish |
| **picante** | pee-**kahn**-teh | spicy |
| **la pimienta** | pee-mee-**yehn**-tah | pepper |
| **el pollo** | **poh**-yoh | chicken |
| **el postre** | **pohs**-treh | dessert |
| **el queso** | **keh**-soh | cheese |
| **el refresco** | reh-**frehs**-koh | soft drink/soda |
| **la sal** | **sahl** | salt |
| **la salsa** | **sahl**-sah | sauce |
| **la sopa** | **soh**-pah | soup |
| **el té** | **teh** | herb tea (usually camomile) |
| **el té negro** | **teh neh**-groh | tea |
| **la torta** | **tohr**-tah | sandwich |
| **las tostadas** | tohs-**tah**-dahs | toast |
| **el vinagre** | vee-**nah**-greh | vinegar |
| **el vino blanco** | **vee**-noh **blahn**-koh | white wine |
| **el vino tinto** | **vee**-noh **teen**-toh | red wine |

## Numbers

| | | |
|---|---|---|
| 0 | **cero** | **seh**-roh |
| 1 | **uno** | **oo**-noh |
| 2 | **dos** | dohs |
| 3 | **tres** | trehs |
| 4 | **cuatro** | **kwa**-troh |
| 5 | **cinco** | **seen**-koh |
| 6 | **seis** | says |
| 7 | **siete** | **see**-eh-teh |
| 8 | **ocho** | **oh**-choh |
| 9 | **nueve** | **nweh**-veh |
| 10 | **diez** | dee-**ehs** |
| 11 | **once** | **ohn**-seh |
| 12 | **doce** | **doh**-seh |
| 13 | **trece** | **treh**-seh |
| 14 | **catorce** | kah-**tohr**-seh |
| 15 | **quince** | **keen**-seh |
| 16 | **dieciséis** | dee-eh-see-**seh-ees** |
| 17 | **diecisiete** | dee-eh-see-see-**eh**-teh |
| 18 | **dieciocho** | dee-eh-see-**oh**-choh |
| 19 | **diecinueve** | dee-eh-see-**nweh**-veh |
| 20 | **veinte** | **veh**-een-teh |
| 21 | **veintiuno** | veh-een-tee-**oo**-noh |
| 22 | **veintidós** | veh-een-tee-**dohs** |
| 30 | **treinta** | **treh**-een-tah |
| 31 | **treinta y uno** | treh-een-tah ee **oo**-noh |
| 40 | **cuarenta** | kwah-**rehn**-tah |
| 50 | **cincuenta** | seen-**kwehn**-tah |
| 60 | **sesenta** | seh-**sehn**-tah |
| 70 | **setenta** | seh-**tehn**-tah |
| 80 | **ochenta** | oh-**chehn**-tah |
| 90 | **noventa** | noh-**vehn**-tah |
| 100 | **cien** | see-**ehn** |
| 101 | **ciento uno** | see-**ehn**-toh **oo**-noh |
| 102 | **ciento dos** | see-**ehn**-toh **dohs** |
| 200 | **doscientos** | dohs-see-**ehn**- tohs |
| 500 | **quinientos** | khee-nee-**ehn**-tohs |
| 700 | **setecientos** | seh-teh-see-**ehn**-tohs |
| 900 | **novecientos** | noh-veh-see-**ehn**-tohs |
| 1,000 | **mil** | meel |
| 1,001 | **mil uno** | **meel oo**-noh |

## Time

| | | |
|---|---|---|
| one minute | **un minuto** | **oon** mee-**noo**-toh |
| one hour | **una hora** | **oo**-nah **oh**-rah |
| half an hour | **media hora** | **meh**-dee-ah **oh**-rah |
| half past one | **la una y media** | lah **oo**-nah ee **meh**-dee-ah |
| Monday | **lunes** | **loo**-nehs |
| Tuesday | **martes** | **mahr**-tehs |
| Wednesday | **miércoles** | mee-**ehr**-koh-lehs |
| Thursday | **jueves** | hoo-**weh**-vehs |
| Friday | **viernes** | vee-**ehr**-nehs |
| Saturday | **sábado** | **sah**-bah-doh |
| Sunday | **domingo** | doh-**meen**-goh |